AMAZON

The Flooded Forest

AMAZON

The Flooded Forest

Michael Goulding

Sterling Publishing Co., Inc.   New York

Library of Congress Cataloging-in-Publication Data

Goulding, Michael.
    Amazon : the flooded forest / Michael Goulding.
        p.   cm.
    Includes index.
    1. Natural history—Amazon River Watershed.   2. Rain forest
ecology—Amazon River Watershed.   3. Rain forests—Amazon River
Watershed.   I. Title.
QH112.G68   1990
508.81'1—dc20   90-39131
                                                          CIP

                    1   3   5   7   9   10   8   6   4   2

            Published in 1990 by Sterling Publishing Company, Inc.
                  387 Park Avenue South, New York, N.Y. 10016
                  Originally published in Great Britain by BBC Books
                          © 1989 by Partridge Films
                  Distributed in Canada by Sterling Publishing
              % Canadian Manda Group, P.O. Box 920, Station U
                     Toronto, Ontario, Canada M8Z 5P9
                   Sterling ISBN 0-8069-7476-1

CONTENTS

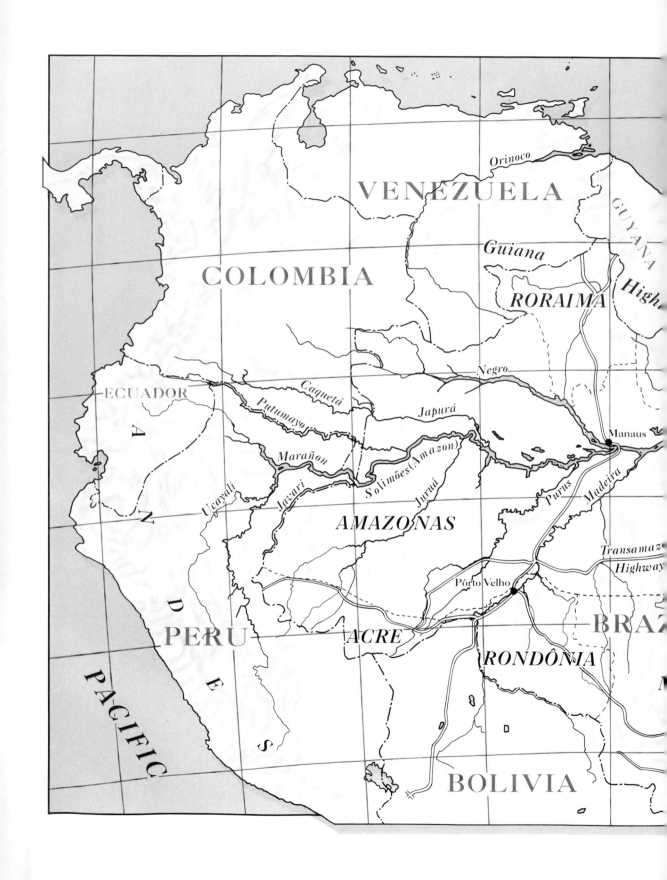

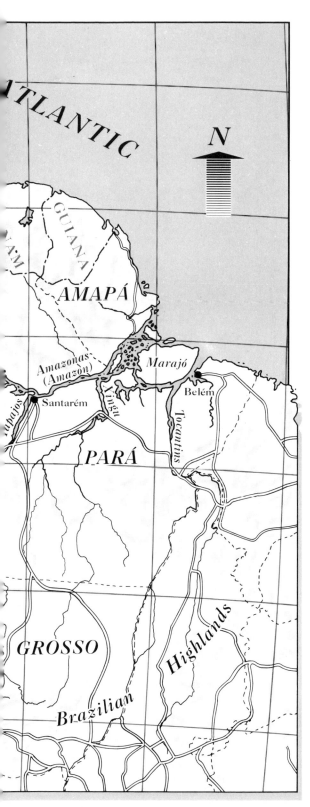

ATLANTIC

N

GUIANA

AM

AMAPÁ

Amazonas
(Amazon)

Marajó

Santarém

Xingu

Belém

apajos

Tocantins

PARÁ

GROSSO

Highlands

Brazilian

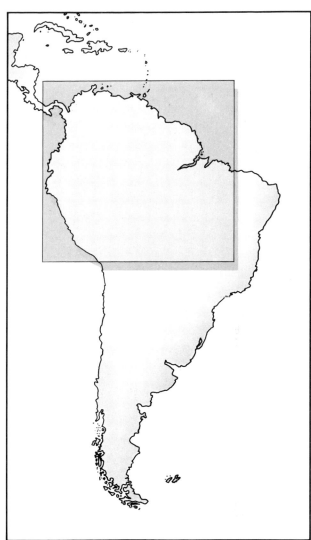

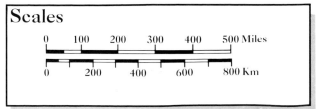

Key

— Highways
—·—·— National Boundaries
— — — Brazilian State Boundaries

Scales

0   100   200   300   400   500 Miles

0   200   400   600   800 Km

ACKNOWLEDGEMENTS

I am first indebted to Michael Rosenberg, executive producer, and Andrea Florence, producer, of Partridge Films Ltd, for suggesting and developing the film and book project.

My research was supported by the Brazilian Government, through its scientific institutions, the National Council of Research and Technological Development (CNPq), National Institute of Amazonian Research (INPA) and the Goeldi Museum. World Wildlife Fund-US has provided much of the financing for my exploration and research in the Amazon since 1979.

I would especially like to thank Thomas E. Lovejoy, Guilherme de La Penha, Charles F. Bennett, Rosemary Lowe-McConnell, Warwick Kerr, Naércio Menezes, Heraldo Britski, Stanley Weitzman, Russel Mittermier and Mark Plotkin for their personal support of my Amazonian research.

The naturalists who have most influenced my thinking on the Amazon are Henry Walter Bates, Alfred Russel Wallace, Richard Spruce, José Veríssimo and Euclides da Cunha.

The scientists to whose Amazonian writings I have most often turned while writing this book are Ghillean Prance (plants), João Murça Pires (plants), Helmut Sick (birds), Harold Sioli (aquatic studies), Márcio Ayres (primates), Nigel Smith (geography), Paulo Vanzolini (reptiles), Ronald Heyer (amphibians), Peter Bayley (aquatic ecology), Wolfgang Junk (aquatic ecology), Robin Best (aquatic mammals), Joaquim Adis (invertebrates) and Hilgard Sternberg (geography).

Martyn Colbeck, Jim Clare, Stephen Foote, Alastair Macewen and Richard Foster, cameramen for the film project, provided either photographic assistance or materials for the book.

Finally, I would like to thank Susan Martineau, Sheila Ableman, Frances Abrahams, Cath Speight and Sarah Spalding of BBC Books for their editorial skills and help.

PREFACE

Amazon: *The Flooded Forest* has been written with two equal purposes in mind. It serves to complement a series of television programmes by the same title made by Partridge Films Ltd for the BBC and it also provides the first modern natural history of Amazonian rivers and the rainforests they flood. The research for the book springs from over 12 years of exploration of the Amazon, coupled with a synthesis of the large body of scientific literature that has become available in the last decade.

As the twenty-first century approaches, it has become apparent that tropical deforestation, river impoundment and pollution will be the environmental echoes that reverberate across the planet from the Amazonian theatre. Herein we will not rally our discussion around the theme of environmental destruction. As an alternative and complementary route, we will explore the beauty and natural history of what so many are now afraid might be lost because of careless management. The films and book are presented as part of an effort to show that the Amazon is a very special place, indeed the greatest celebration of the ecology of life that the planet has ever known.

Most voyagers and naturalists to the Amazon travel on the rivers, for the waterways are nature's highways through the rainforest. These rivers not only cut through the rainforest, but during the floods actually invade much of it as rising waters spill over the banks. The world of the flooded forest combines the delights of the upland forest with the aquatic and amphibious mysteries of the rivers. The flooded forest is the most curious feature of the Amazon because it is nature's combined response to terrestrial and aquatic life. It is the habitat where the most kinds of life meet and interact, in other words, a type of centre ring where one of the great nature acts on Earth takes place. This work explores not only flooded forest life, but also the many curious plants and animals found in river channels, lakes and in the area where the Amazon meets the Atlantic Ocean.

The book has been written in non-technical prose but with scientific fact, as best as it is presently understood, always in mind. Most of the reliable literature dealing with the natural history of the Amazon is scattered far and wide in scientific journals in various languages, thus citations are neither made in the text nor is a bibliography included. The reader who wishes to explore the more technical literature is referred to two excellent recent volumes that contain large bibliographies on many Amazonian subjects. These are *Amazonia* (Pergamon Press, Oxford and New York, 1985, edited by G. T. Prance & T. E. Lovejoy) and *The Amazon: Limnology and Landscape Ecology of a Mighty Tropical River and its Basin* (Dr W. Junk Publishers, Dordrecht and Boston, 1984, edited by H. Sioli).

CHAPTER ONE

TIME

ON THE

AMAZON

Sir Arthur Conan Doyle, while ascending the steep slopes of his towering imagination, discovered a Lost World on an ancient Mesozoic tableland rising out of the Amazonian rainforest. There Professor Challenger, science's most fiery, sarcastic and lovable explorer, guided by the same brilliance as his literary brother, Sherlock Holmes, investigated surviving giant reptiles and ancient plants left as lonely reminders of an act that had been swept aside in the march of Earth's time. Sir Arthur chose exactly the right geological era to investigate the Amazon of the past. For it was in the Mesozoic Era that the Amazonian stage was radically reset for all that has since followed.

When the heavy steps of dinosaurs still pounded along some ancient Amazonian shore, the giant river and land had yet to resemble anything we now find on our maps. Around 80–90 million years ago, or just before the Mesozoic dinosaurs became extinct, South America and Africa began to split apart and divide Gondwanaland, that ancient landmass that included not only our two largest tropical continents but also parts of southern Asia, Australia and Antarctica. Where Gondwanaland ruptured to its west, a new ocean, the Atlantic, appeared and separated South America completely from Africa. South America in effect became a giant island floating slowly westward on the Earth's crust. The whole process is referred to as continental drift. Of all the tropical theatres of evolution, South America claimed the most diverse cast of species. This is in large part because the Amazon Basin provided ideal conditions for the radiation of life into an almost unbelievable number of niches.

At about the same time that South America and Africa began to go their separate continental ways, that 'most abominable mystery', as Charles Darwin called it, spread across the planet, geologically speaking, like a fire before the wind. The flowering plants had arrived. Today the Amazon is quite unimaginable without flowering plants, the botanical foundation of the rainforest. What the Amazon was like in its pre-flower period can only be guessed, as the sedimentary basin, and its humid climate, have not been kind to fossils. Based on fossil evidence from other South American regions, the large basin was probably largely clothed in cycads and other gymnosperm-like plants and many different kinds of ferns, some of them reaching tree-like proportions. Today most of the gymnosperm species, such as pines and firs, are restricted to the high latitudes or to lofty elevations. Many fern species are still found in the Amazon, but none are giants. Only one gymnosperm group survived the flower onslaught, though this was not a tree but a curious climbing vine. These *Gnetum* vines literally hang on to the flowering plants for their lives. In a way the *Gnetum* vines may be seen as the only live prisoners that the flowering plants took among the gymnosperms whose land and water they conquered.

Not only did the flowering plants bring a new botanical nature to the Amazon, but they also opened up millions of niches for tiny animals, especially insects, and by so doing also led to an increase in their own diversity as highly specific plant and animal interactions evolved. No one knows for sure exactly where flowering plants first evolved. It is usually thought to be somewhere in the tropics. It could have been in the Amazon as easily as anywhere else, and there perhaps along a swamp or river where the gentle interplay of light, moisture and temperature encouraged the first plant to bloom. About 30 000 flowering plant species are known from the Amazon Basin, the world's richest region, which is one-third of the total for all of South America and nearly three times the number claimed by all of Europe. We still have no realistic idea of how many insect species there might be in the Amazonian rainforest, though it is probably in the millions. All of these, in one way or another, are ecologically linked to flowering plants.

The third great event in Amazonian history – subsequent to the splitting of the continents and the appearance of flowering plants – was the rise of the Andean Mountains. The major rise of the Andes took place only in the last 15 million years when the South American continental plate, slowly floating westwards on the Earth's mantle, collided with the so-called Nazca plate which now underlies much of the Eastern Pacific along the coast of South America. As the Nazca plate slid underneath the South American plate, the zone of contact was pushed upwards, thus commencing Andean mountain building. Until the rise of the Andes the Amazon River flowed westwards and into the Pacific. The new mountains, however, robbed the Amazon of its only outlet to an ocean, for the Brazilian and Guiana Highlands were still joined to the east and prevented any drainage to the Atlantic. The Amazon in effect became the largest lake and swamp ecosystem the planet Earth has ever known.

If you are unfortunate enough to step on an Amazonian stingray, one of the most painful creatures in all of the great river system because of its venomous sting, you may look westwards and curse the Andes instead of your carelessness. As the Andes rose, inland seas, cut off from the Pacific, were transformed into freshwater lakes. It was in these waterbodies that stingrays and some other animal groups evolved the adaptations to live in South American freshwaters. Today there are more than 20 species of stingrays in Amazonian waters, and their nearest marine relatives are found only in the Pacific, that is, far across the Andes.

It was not until about 10 million years ago, in the Pliocene period, that the Amazon River finally managed to excavate its present course eastwards through the low-lying valley separating the Brazilian and Guiana Highlands. The impounded lake and swamp landscape was transformed into a river and rainforest ecosystem linked to the Atlantic.

The last major geological event that transformed the Amazon into what we see today was the locking and unlocking of huge amounts of water by the polar ice caps. With cooler global temperatures the ice caps grew and consequently reduced sea levels. For example, about 18 000 years ago sea levels were nearly 130 metres lower than today. During low sea level periods Amazonian rivers ran faster and were able to excavate their soft riverbeds and valley walls. Today when you fly along the Amazon you will notice that the lower reaches of most of the tributaries look like lakes rather than rivers. This is because these tributaries have not filled their riverbeds and floodplains with sediments since they were scoured out by the torrential waters that raced towards a lowered Ice Age Atlantic. The Amazon River was also greatly excavated during Ice Age periods, but subsequently Andean sediments transported downstream have built up its floodplain and raised the level of its riverbed. Today the average depth of the Amazon River during the floods is 30–50 metres. Only in two places in the Amazon – the lower Rio Negro and middle Rio Amazonas – are there depths greater than 100 metres. These sites represent fossil canyons formed during Pleistocene Ice Ages. If you could sit on the bottom of the lower Rio Negro in front of the city of Manaus, some 2000 kilometres upstream of the Atlantic, you would be 60 metres below sea level in the deepest part of the channel.

Not only was sea level much lower than today, but later it was also considerably higher and with quite different effects on the Amazon. Around 6000 years ago sea levels reached some 130 metres higher than at present. The Amazon River valley, including the lower courses of its tributaries, was drowned with freshwater that was dammed back by the Atlantic. At this time the Amazon undoubtedly looked more like a lake, some 20–50 kilometres in width, than a river. The Amazon still reaches this width during its high water period, but the floodplains are now high enough to support rainforest, although it is inundated for much of the year. The river channel between the floodplains on either side now averages 2–5 kilometres.

When entering the Amazon from the Atlantic one will first be struck by how dirty the waters appear to be. The local peoples refer to the Amazon and its tributaries carrying heavy quantities of Andean sediments as whitewater rivers, though they are really more *café au lait* in colour. When you drink a glass of unfiltered Amazon river water, you are also eating a piece of the Andes because of the high content of suspended solids that have been brought downstream from the mountains.

If it were possible to sit on the bottom of the Amazon River and see across its bed one would witness giant sand and silt dunes being rolled downstream by the fast current. Some of these dunes, as shown by recorded echo-grams, reach over 10 metres in height. Most of the sediments are washed out to sea, though silt deposits near the mouth of the Amazon are over 2000 metres thick. In the abyss off the mouth of the Amazon, the river's sediments have been deposited in an area the size of the British Isles and form an enormous submarine cone over 11 000 metres high. If this cone were somehow placed on land, then it would be our planet's highest mountain.

As we continue our journey up the muddy Amazon we will meet the second river type, or the clearwater tributaries whose headwaters rise on the Brazilian and Guiana Highlands. The middle and upper reaches of these tributaries have many cataracts and waterfalls that mark the rocky presence of South America's most ancient geology. Rivers such as the Xingu and Tapajós drain massive areas of little erosion, thus their waters are relatively transparent, soft and a pleasure to bathe in if you do not mind the tons of mercury that are now being poured into them from gold mining operations. Once we pass the turbid Rio Madeira some 1200 kilometres upstream, the muddy and clearwater tributaries give way to a majority of blackwater rivers in the Amazonian Lowlands. These are the most peculiar of all the Amazon's rivers because of their dark yet clean waters. To understand the origin of these strange blackwaters we must consider the nature of the Amazonian Lowlands.

The Amazonian Lowlands, splaying out in a westerly direction, forms the greatest sedimentary basin on Earth. The towering mountains whose reduced remnants are now the Brazilian and Guiana Highlands were laid largely to rest as sands and clays on the Amazonian floor. Like a giant vortex, the Amazonian Lowlands, sinking under its own weight, sucked these sands and clays downwards before many of them could be transported away to sea. The huge depression has sunk so far into the Earth's crust that in places the sediments exceed 4000 metres in thickness.

The large amount of sand deposited in the Amazonian Lowlands led to the development of the blackwater rivers. The sandy soils of the Amazon Basin are

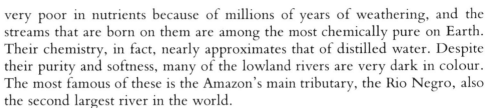

very poor in nutrients because of millions of years of weathering, and the streams that are born on them are among the most chemically pure on Earth. Their chemistry, in fact, nearly approximates that of distilled water. Despite their purity and softness, many of the lowland rivers are very dark in colour. The most famous of these is the Amazon's main tributary, the Rio Negro, also the second largest river in the world.

Rio Negro water could pass in colour for Guinness or dark tea. It is more acidic than coca-cola, but better for you. The peculiar colour of the Rio Negro, and other large Amazonian blackwater rivers, is due to the heavy input of incompletely decomposed organic matter. The sandy soils are too poor in micro-organisms, and especially fungi, bacteria and invertebrates, to transform the organic matter into its constituent chemical end-products. In addition, the large quantity of organic compounds that finds its way into the ground water is not filtered out by the sand as might be expected. Sand, unlike clay, does not have the chemical properties that allow it to bind the organic end-products of forest decomposition. The organic overload is thus carried into the streams and rivers and renders them dark in colour.

Before the rise of the Andes the Amazon River itself may have been, at least during parts of its geological history, a blackwater river somewhat similar to the Rio Negro as seen today. This is suggested by the fact that most of the Amazon's large western non-Andean tributaries are today blackwater rivers. The Amazon's most beautiful fish, the famous neon and cardinal of the aquarium trade, also seem to point to the once blackwater of the main river.

The neon and cardinal undoubtedly evolved from a common but now extinct ancestor that was widely distributed in the western part of the Amazon Basin, and there mostly to blackwater. The cardinal is now only found in the Rio Negro and some of its tributaries, whereas the neon lives much further west in the general vicinity of the Brazilian-Peruvian-Colombian border. Today the Amazon, issuing from the high Andes to the west, separates these brilliant relatives because they cannot survive in the muddy water of the main river, which they would have to do in order to disperse into the other's territory. Their beauty, however, has bought them tickets to the far corners of the aquarium world. Today from Tokyo to London to New York, Amazonian neons and cardinals swim under fluorescent light in millions of living-rooms. They are ichthyological gifts from the world of Amazonian blackwater, and from the sands that produce them.

We may now put the whitewater, clearwater and blackwater contributions together to arrive at the geographical total of our planet's largest river. The Amazon delivers about one-fifth of the freshwater that is discharged annually into the oceans by all the world's rivers. Its discharge is 5 times that of the Zaire (Congo), 10 times that of the Mississippi and 3500 times that of the Thames.

 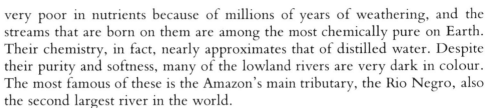

Though the Amazon is by far the largest river in the world because of its enormous discharge, it is not usually taken to be the longest. The Nile-Kagera stretches some 6700 kilometres through north-eastern Africa, whereas the Amazon can claim no more than about 6500 kilometres from its furthest point in the Andes to the Atlantic. One fact that is often forgotten, however, is that during the floods the Amazon River pushes far out to sea, and if we add this dimension then it is probably longer than the Nile-Kagera.

The animals now found in the Amazon had several geographical origins due to South America's complex geological history. Before exploring specific river and forest habitats, we will first trace the evolutionary paths of some of the most interesting animal groups that now populate the Amazon.

If we allow the imagination to wade back in time into an Amazonian Paleozoic or early Mesozoic swamp, more than 150 million years ago, we would recognise many insect groups though very few of the vertebrate animals would resemble any of the modern species. Perhaps the most notable exception would be Earth's most admirable survivor in freshwater, the lungfish.

Lungfish were widespread well before the continents began to drift apart. The South American lungfish is not restricted to the Amazon, but it is most common there. As their name indicates, lungfish have a lung, a novel air-breathing organ, for the Paleozoic that is, that evolved from an air-bladder. They were probably the first animals to evolve this air-breathing organ. The ability to breathe atmospheric air is undoubtedly the single most important factor accounting for their survival for so long. Today if you wade through a shrinking Amazon floodplain pool during the dry season, where the stench of swamp gas that is stirred up will trace your steps, and the fetid smell reminds you that little if any oxygen is left in the mud-hole, you may be lucky enough to see a lungfish stick its head out of water for a gulp of air. The eternal and satisfied smile its deeply slit mouth emits seems to be a reminder from one whose relatives have witnessed the renting of continents and weathered all the geological seasons that tropical life itself has confronted. In comparison, the short evolutionary span of our own species begs for humility before the altar of lungfish time.

Before Africa and South America underwent continental drift, there evolved a group of freshwater fish in which the anterior vertebrae of the backbone became fused together to support delicate bones. These bones were then able to transmit sounds from the air-bladder to the inner ear of the fish. Because freshwater is less dense than seawater, sound waves do not travel so well in it, thus the acoustical specialists that evolved had a great advantage over other fish. The characins (piranhas, neons and many others), catfish and electric knife-fish are the acoustical specialists of the Amazon and, though they look very different, we know that they evolved from the same ancient ancestor because they all possess the modified vertebral column for sound gathering. Today they account for well over 80 per cent of the 2500–3000 fish species of the Amazon, the world's richest ichthyological region. The Amazon alone probably has about 10 times as many fish species as all of Europe and 2–3 times as many as the Zaire (Congo) system.

The reptilian fauna of Amazonian rivers is long past its heyday, for few of the Mesozoic groups survived except in Sir Arthur Conan Doyle's *Lost World.* The side-necked turtles are among the few survivors from Gondwanaland days. Before the formation of the Atlantic Ocean, the crocodilian faunas of the South American and African landmasses, of course then still joined, were very similar. Many of these were reminiscent of the gavials now found only in Southern Asia and associated islands, though some of the species were giants, reaching over 10 metres in length. The gavial-like crocodilians became extinct in South America and were replaced in the Amazon by the caimans, whose geographical origins are still uncertain. Of living relatives caimans are more closely related to alligators than crocodiles. Caimans, however, should be called neither alligators nor crocodiles, for they are quite different.

Constricting snakes, of which the anaconda is the Amazon's prime example, have a long geological history reaching well back into the Mesozoic Era. None of the modern groups, however, appear to have been present when the continents separated, and Amazonian species are very different from Old World counterparts, such as the pythons. The most diverse group of snakes in the Amazon belong to the family Colubridae. These are usually called common snakes because they are the ones most often seen. Many of them resemble poisonous snakes, but none are venomous. Several venomous snake families, however, such as the corals, evolved from colubrid ancestors. The venomous South American snakes evolved subsequent to the splitting of the continents, perhaps in response to the appearance of many kinds of new prey animals, such as small mammals. The most dangerous and numerous of Amazonian venomous snakes, the pit vipers, evolved mostly for a terrestrial existence, though many of the species are common along the water's edge. None of the Amazonian pit vipers can be considered aquatic, though all of the species associated with the water's edge can swim well if need be.

Semi-aquatic iguana and teiid lizards, many reaching over a metre in length, have most likely been falling out of the tops of riverine forest trees and crashing into the water whenever danger presented itself, since the Mesozoic Era. Today there are about four or five common semi-aquatic lizards in the Amazon.

The Amazon's oldest amphibians are caecilians, a group that originated not on the southern island of Italy, as a similar pronunciation might suggest, but somewhere in Gondwanaland. Caecilians are legless amphibians, and the most common groups in the Amazon are aquatic, look like large black worms or snakes, and stay hidden in the roots of floating vegetation.

Aquatic frogs are very poorly represented in the Amazon, most likely because fish have undergone such a dramatic diversification and the amphibians cannot compete with them for space and food. Also, frogs in general would be relatively easy prey for the many species of predatory fish of the Amazon. The most ancient aquatic frogs are the *Pipa* toads, species that spend most of their time hidden beneath leaf-litter. By far the greatest diversity of frogs and toads associated with Amazonian rivers is found just above the water's surface on floating or forest vegetation. Only the tadpoles are aquatic.

The Amazon is the richest bird region in the world, claiming just over 900 species. Many new bird families evolved once South America became an island, though none of these belongs to aquatic or semi-aquatic families. Aquatic birds are in general widely distributed and most are migratory, thus the chances of unique families evolving is much less than for terrestrial species. The only unique avian origin associated with the development of the Amazon river system is the hoatzin, a bird roughly resembling artistic reconstructions of the Jurassic period's most famous fossil, the *Archaeopteryx*. The hoatzin, however, probably descended from a cuckoo-like ancestor, and is far removed in evolution from the ancient *Archaeopteryx*. Rainforest, rather than water, was the most important factor that led to South America's unique bird fauna. Migratory birds, as is the case with most of the Earth, move largely in a north-south direction or vice versa according to the seasons. No species migrate between South America and Africa.

Mammals appeared before Gondwanaland separated into the various continents, and the South American island took with it only three major groups, which were a diverse range of marsupials, edentates (sloths, armadillos and anteaters) and some archaic hoofed beasts. Most of the marsupials were eventually replaced by placental mammals, that is, those whose young, like our own species, develop in the uterus, and are linked to the mother by a placenta or afterbirth. Most of the placental mammals now found in South America migrated there when it became connected to Central America via the Panamanian Isthmus 3–4 million years ago. The only marsupial in the Amazon to evolve an aquatic life was the water opossum, but just where it originated is uncertain. It does not seem to penetrate very deeply into the Amazon Basin, and perhaps it is only a recent invader into this system.

Most of the South American hoofed mammals became extinct in recent geological times. Tapirs are the most ancient group of hoofed species to survive in South America. The Brazilian tapir is common in the Amazon. It is also the only native hoofed animal that commonly enters Amazonian waters, mostly for bathing and escaping predators, but occasionally for feeding as well.

Three important groups of Amazonian mammals – monkeys, certain kinds of rodents (capybara, paca and agouti), and bats – first appear in the fossil record about 40 million years ago, that is, when South America was still an island. The best guess is that they evolved from immigrants that somehow made it across the seas separating South America from either Africa or North and Central America.

At least one monkey species, the white bald uakari (pronounced wah-car-ee), appears to have evolved as a consequence of Amazonian floodplains, the only habitat where it lives. The largest rodent in the world, the capybara, is also the Amazon's most aquatic. The lush meadows of water hyacinths, grasses and other aquatic plants which evolved on Amazonian floodplains provide capybaras with a large food resource, on which only they, of the rodents, have become highly specialized feeders.

The Amazon has received three mammalian immigrants from the seas, or at least their ancestors were marine. One factor that might have encouraged marine manatees to colonize freshwater was global cooling during the Oligocene period (38–26 million years ago) when seagrass beds retreated, but floodplain herbaceous plants in the rivers were abundant. The manatees turned to the available food source. Just how they got into the Amazon system, however, is unclear since the main river did not empty into the Atlantic when manatees first began to appear in freshwater. Perhaps they colonized from the Pacific, though they are no longer found along that side of South America. The West Indian and Amazonian manatees are found together in the Amazon River mouth area. Although the West Indian species moves into the Orinoco system, it does not enter the Amazon.

The primitive river dolphin found in the Amazon and Orinoco systems was derived from an ancestral marine group that was widespread along tropical continental coasts. River dolphins today are found in China, the Indian subcontinent area and northern South America. A marine relative also lives along the Atlantic coast of southern South America. None of the species moves between sea- and freshwater. The South American river dolphin appears to have got trapped in Amazonian freshwater when the Andes rose and it was cut off from marine ancestors. The freshwater species that arose in this western sea or seas then dispersed eastwards and northwards. One population, however, has probably been trapped since about the time the species first evolved, and this is in the Rio Madeira headwaters of the Bolivian Lowlands. A large number of cataracts in the upper Rio Madeira separates the Bolivian Lowlands from the main part of the Amazon Basin and thus makes dispersal difficult. Today the Bolivian and main Amazonian dolphin populations have slightly different shapes, the result of geographical isolation that has prevented interbreeding.

The other cetacean species found in the Amazon belongs to the main family of dolphins, the Delphinidae. There are over 30 species of these dolphins in the oceans. The *tucuxi*-dolphin appears to have entered the Amazon only after it began to flow to the Atlantic in recent geological times. It has a close relative, which is found in the Amazon estuary, along the South American Atlantic coast and in some rivers other than the Amazon. However, as with the pair of manatee species, these two dolphins do not inhabit the same rivers, except in a limited area of the Amazon estuary.

The last major event in the evolution of mammals now associated with the Amazon was the joining of South and Central America at the Isthmus of Panama. This joining provided a bridge for northern immigrants, especially terrestrial and arboreal animals. The first northern mammals began to reach South America about 7 million years ago as waif, or chance, immigrants across the narrow sea still separating the two landmasses. Coatis, racoon-like mammals, were among the first northern immigrants to reach the Amazonian rainforest. Of the terrestrial mammals that originated in the north and subsequently dispersed into South America, there are the cats, various rodents, deer and peccaries. The only aquatic mammals that migrated from Central America and reached the Amazon were the giant river otter, or at least a close relative from which it was derived, and the smaller Neotropical river otter, and this colonization took place only in the last 3 million years.

Finally, *Homo sapiens* followed late on the tail of the other mammals and migrated from the north and across the Isthmus of Panama and into South America at least 20 000 years ago and reached the Amazon no later than 10 000 years before the present. The first humans in the Amazon Basin were Amerindians. Europeans, and the African slaves they brought with them, began to colonize the Amazon Basin in the sixteenth century. European colonization exterminated most of the native peoples through disease and enslavement. Colonization from the Old World was largely over by the end of the nineteenth century, with the notable exception of Japanese immigrants who began to arrive in the early part of the twentieth century. Since the 1970s, grandiose rainforest development schemes and gold rushes have spurred waves of migration to the Amazon from various South American countries, Brazil being the most important. Riding the crests of these population waves are high birth rates. Other than himself, Man has also introduced a large number of exotic plants and animals. The most important introduced plants are bananas and pasture grasses. Introduced live-stock, especially cattle and water buffalo, have been the principal animals used in Man's attempt to beef up the Amazonian rainforest.

◆ CHAPTER TWO ◆

FLOODS

IN THE

FOREST

As the floods flow to sea through the Amazonian Lowlands they cannot be contained within the mere limits of the river channels. The waters pour over the channel levees and invade the huge floodplain areas that have developed over thousands of years as a consequence of minimal relief and river course changes in the fluvial valleys. The flood invasion is seasonal because the distribution of rainfall is seasonal.

The three principal features of Amazonian floodplains are the flooded forests, open waterbodies usually called lakes, and floating meadows of herbaceous plants. The *igapó*, as the flooded forest is called, is one of the most peculiar features of the Amazon. The *igapó* forest has been so successful in colonizing the floodplains that its total extent is far greater than that of the lakes and meadows taken together. Almost all areas of the floodplain that are less than about 12 metres deep at the peak of the floods support rainforest. The flooded forest has different tree species to its adjacent upland counterpart – the so-called *terra firme* rainforest – and its unique flora has undoubtedly evolved as a result of special adaptations needed to survive long periods of inundation.

There are stretches along some of the larger rivers, such as the meandering Purus and Juruá, where during the floods one could enjoy the surrealistic experience of paddling a small dugout canoe for several hundred kilometres upstream or downstream without ever abandoning the shade of the *igapó*. Of course, one should only do this with a native paddleman, otherwise it would be very easy to get lost far into a maze of flooded forest that might be over 10 kilometres in width from the river channel to the *terra firme*.

The flooded forest offers two advantages to the naturalist that upland forest cannot. First, water provides a natural highway through an otherwise difficult

environment to negotiate, and second, the floods provide a far-reaching platform, with the help of a canoe, that perches the observer above the understoreys
of the forest and sometimes within reach of the canopy. The most striking sensa-
tion one feels upon first entering the *igapó* at the height of the floods, and from
the vantage point of a canoe, is the closeness of the canopy above. As one scrapes
past trees, it is possible to probe into giant bromeliads, pluck canopy fruits,
twang the threads of spider gossamers built between upper storey trees, sidle by
hanging wasp nests and enjoy any number of other experiences that are usually
impossible from the forest floor perspective alone. But if we want to see the
flooded forest understorey at this time of year, we will need diving equipment
since, by looking into the water or taking a depth sounding, we might find that it
is inundated to a depth of 10 metres or more.

Amazon flooded forest occupies at least 100 000 square kilometres, and perhaps half that again if we knew its extent along the tens of thousands of small
streams that serpentine their way below the rainforest canopy. Though flooded
forest can only claim about 2 per cent of the total Amazonian rainforest, this
nevertheless represents an area larger than England. Imagine paddling a canoe
from London to any point in England, all the time beneath canopy shade, and
the immensity of the Amazon's flooded forest can be grasped.

Although, because of its extent, the Amazon flooded forest is singular compared to similar formations in other river systems of the world, it is by no means
homogeneous. Within it there are several kinds of flooded forest. The seasonally flooded forest is by far the most extensive type, and it is found along all of
the rivers of the Amazonian Lowlands because of the extensive development of
floodplains. This type of forest can be inundated for 3–11 months each year,
depending on local floodplain topography and the intensity of the annual
floods. In general, however, the seasonal floods cover vast expanses of the
floodplains for an average of 4–7 months each year.

Seasonally flooded forest gives way to tidal forest where influence of the
tides is met about 300 kilometres upriver. Until saltwater dominates, the tidal
flooded forest has largely the same stature and species as the seasonally inundated counterpart further upstream. The tidal flooded forest, of course, is not
inundated on a seasonal basis, but rather twice daily with the rise of the oceanic
tides. Its fruiting and flowering behaviour, however, is much the same as that of
the seasonally flooded forest.

Irregularly flooded forest is most associated with streams that are inundated
whenever there are heavy rains. The restricted stream valleys are unable to
accommodate the run-off that rushes into them, and hence the rainforest fringing them is flooded. The species composition of this forest, however, is usually
the same as the adjacent upland communities, for inundation is never long
enough to require special adaptations to flooding. Each of the many thousands

of small streams flowing out of Amazonian rainforest forms a bristle in a giant ecological broom. Stream waters sweep through the fringing forests and in effect transport much organic matter into the aquatic ecosystem. This organic material is especially important to foodchains in the lowland streams because they are too poor in nutrients, and too shaded, to produce large quantities of algae or aquatic herbaceous plants to fuel the animal communities that live in them.

Swamp forest is semi-permanently, and occasionally permanently, inundated and exists in low-lying areas that are poorly drained, usually because of a high water table. Tree diversity is greatly reduced in Amazonian swamp forests because few species can tolerate being permanently waterlogged. Palms usually dominate in these waterlogged forests.

Along rivers, such as the Amazon and Madeira, that receive annual injections of rich Andean silt the flooded forest reaches its most towering heights, often matching those of the adjacent *terra firme*. Some of the emergent trees above the upper canopy can reach 40 metres in height, and are probably several hundred years old. The kapok, or silk-cotton tree, is the most majestic floodplain tree. Before it was largely destroyed along the Amazon River for cheap box timber, it was relatively evenly spaced along the levees. It is still common on some of the tributaries, such as the Purus and lower Madeira. Standing on giant buttressed roots, the straight stem pokes above the upper canopy at which point the kapok's crown splays out under the support of horizontal limbs that often exceed 30 metres in length. With its crown largely above the main upper canopy, the kapok embraces the full thrust of the winds sweeping over the top of the rainforest. In contrast to most flooded forest plants, the fruits ripen during the low water period, at which time the leaves also drop to allow an even freer flow-through of wind. The capsular fruits split open and release small pieces of cotton-like material, in which are embedded small but hard seeds. The kapok cottonballs are wafted about by the wind until they fall to the ground or often into the river where they are rafted downstream until they drift ashore or are destroyed by hungry seed-eating fish.

Shoreline plants, usually shrubs, are often completely submerged for 7–10 months each year. They must flower and fruit in the short period of time that they are above water. Understorey plants, which include mostly seedlings and saplings of less than 3 metres height, spend much if not most of their immature life underwater. In deeply shaded areas where seedling and sapling growth is limited by poor light, thus hindering photosynthesis, a decade or two of life may be spent in a largely submerged state. With the seasonal draining of the flooded forests as river levels fall each year, the seedlings, saplings and other understorey plants capture whatever sunlight energy they can to invest in their growth.

How flooded forests survive such long periods of inundation is still in large part a scientific mystery. No universal adaptations are obvious, such as seasonal leaf fall during the floods, which theoretically might encourage a slower rate of growth. It is obvious, however, that the flooded forest communities are adapted to survive unscathed despite the absence of oxygen in the root zone. Roots require oxygen for respiration. This is why most plants cannot live in habitats where there is poor drainage, that is, where there are no air spaces in the soil. Water below about 2–3 metres contains almost no oxygen. Even where oxygen is found near the bottom, it is used up in decomposition processes. Aerial roots originating above the floodline are found in only a minority of flooded forest tree species. Though this adaptation would appear to be an excellent way to get around the root oxygen problem, it has not evolved in very many plant groups. Most likely there are other, yet unknown but more efficient, adaptations for overcoming the root oxygen problem. The ability to tolerate long flooding periods is probably hidden in biochemical adaptations that promote respiration, rather than in any gross structural traits, such as aerial roots. Many of the flooded forest plant species probably have physiological adaptations for making the most out of poor light levels. One indication of this is that most of the trees retain their leaves for months at a time even when they are completely flooded. Some photosynthesis, then, takes place underwater.

Most plants in the flooded forest are pollinated by animals. The relatively dense rainforest vegetation largely eliminates wind as an effective pollinator. Animals are more reliable pollinators while insects are undoubtedly the most important and birds, monkeys, rodents and other vertebrates are involved as well. However, few of these last cases have been studied.

As in *terra firme* forest, *igapó* flowers show a large number of specialized structures either to attract pollinators or to prevent unwanted visitors from penetrating the blooms. The flowers of the *castanharanas*, a group of plants common in floodplain forests and related to the famous Brazil-nut tree, are bee-pollinated and have a type of spring-hood that coils over the stamens in the same general area where nectar is produced. In this case, only carpenter and a few other bee groups can lift the hood up to a point where they have access to the nectar. When they do this, of course, they are brushed with pollen that will fertilize another flower of the same species when the large bees visit it in their feeding rounds.

Most flowering plant species produce nectar to attract pollinators. Some, however, have special oil-producing glands instead of nectar. In the Amazon flooded forests the *socoró* tree, a member of the Melastomataceae family, is one of these. Mining bees (Anthophoridae) are the most specialized pollinators of *socoró* plants because their legs are adapted to transport flower oil. *Socoró*-visiting bees collect the flower oil, which is high in fatty compounds, and take it to their hives. They also collect pollen but this is done through a process called 'buzz pollination'. The pollen is not easy to get at because the short slits on the flower's anthers make it inaccessible. After landing on the flowers the bees vibrate ('buzz') their flight muscles, an activity that is easily heard if you are nearby, and this causes the small pollen grains to propel upwards and out of the diminutive anther slits. In the hives the oil is mixed with pollen to prepare the bed where the female will deposit her eggs. After birth the larval bees then feed on the oil-pollen concoction.

Little is yet known about beetle pollination of flooded forest trees, though this group is so common that one suspects it is of great importance. Some or most of the wild soursops (*Annona*), another abundant plant group of the floodplains, are probably pollinated, at least in part, by beetles. About an hour after sunset *Annona* flowers produce an intensive odour attracting both beetles and flies which push their way through the petals. There, the insects become more or less self-imprisoned since they could leave if they wanted to. Once the flower is penetrated, the stigmas and stamens fall off inside and the pollen is released, some attaching itself to the insects. The petals then begin dropping off and the insects, covered with pollen, are released to visit another flower the next day. Sometimes the beetles copulate within the flowers, and when this happens they become even more covered with pollen.

River banks differ most greatly from the interior of the flooded forest because of their full exposure to sunlight. Rank walls of climbing vines often cover the forest's edge where it meets the river. Among the common vines seen are those of the gourd family Cucurbitaceae, whose large flowers stand out sharply against the otherwise rather homogeneous green backdrop of the forest. There are many species but most have red, yellow or white flowers and most are pollinated by butterflies. Male and female flowers, which are very similar in appearance, are produced on different vines. When the male and female vines are intertwined, it is difficult to tell that they are actually separate plants. The male flowers only last for about a day before they fall off. Butterflies, especially the helicons, visit the vines for the pollen in the male flowers. The butterflies, however, cannot distinguish between male and female flowers. When a female flower is mistakenly entered it is then pollinated.

A potential case of a plant that is pollinated by moths is the piranha-tree, a floodplain species renowned for its extremely heavy wood and whose seeds taint the flesh of the animals that feed on them. The piranha-tree is a member of the euphorb family, to which also belongs the famous rubber tree. During the floods the piranha-tree produces huge seed crops that are fed on by many fish species, though piranhas are not usually among these. So why is it named the piranha-tree? Strangely enough the tree's name is derived from its association with a noctuid moth. The end of the piranha-tree fruiting season occurs after the peak of the floods and when water level begins falling. At this time the tree loses its leaves and a new crop appears almost immediately. The new crop becomes blackened with hordes of moth caterpillars devouring the young leaves. The caterpillars fall into the water in large numbers, usually because of storms. Many fish species snap up the caterpillars when they fall into the water, but large black piranhas make such a commotion under the trees, attacking both the moth larvae and the fish feeding on them, that the piranha-tree has been so designated in Amazonian folk botany.

Once the piranha-trees are stripped of their leaves, the remaining caterpillars pupate and retreat within cocoons suspended from the branches. The piranha-tree now produces a second, and unmolested, crop of new leaves. Adult moths appear at about the time of flowering, and they are the suspected pollinators. In short, the piranha-tree 'pays' the noctuid moths one leaf-crop per year to guarantee pollination.

Insects, both in terms of diversity and numbers, are the most successful rainforest animals. The great diversity of insects and flowering plants evolved together, and each depends on the other as we have seen in terms of pollination. No one knows for sure how many insect species there might be in the Amazonian rainforest, by far the richest entomological region in the world, though whatever the number, it is in the millions.

Amazonian flooded forests have provided both opportunities and challenges to insects. Studies made thus far indicate that insects represent about 90 per cent of all arthropods (the jointed invertebrate animals) found in flooded forests, followed by spiders and relatives at 9 per cent, the remaining 1 per cent comprising various other groups. Ground-dwelling insects face the greatest challenge in flooded forests because most of them are not adapted to undergo a submerged phase, thus the annual floods 'chase' them up the trees or on to higher ground. Flooding precludes insects that are purely ground-dwelling. Many of the insects, and other arthropods as well, that use the forest floor during the dry season pass the floods under loose bark in the emerged parts of trees or in bromeliads and other attached plants. During the floods bromeliads become so heavily packed with arthropods that they attract insect-feeding birds and other animals.

With the beginning of the rains, but prior to actual flooding, insect activity and emergence increases on the flooded forest floor, and continues to do so until inundation takes place. Flies, beetles, ants, pseudo-scorpions, spiders and symphylans (centipede-like animals) are frequent on the dry *igapó* floor. At the beginning of the rainy season the number of flying adult insects decreases on the tree trunks, though nymphs can become more common. Non-flying soil arthropods begin to migrate upwards to the trunk and canopy layers, with spiders, millipedes and centipedes being especially common. Most arthropod groups appear to migrate upwards before the actual inundation starts, and their movements are spurred by rising wetness on the forest floor, caused by rising groundwater, and increasing relative humidity in the lower trunk region of the forest. Some groups, however, wait it out, and only leave the forest floor when it is flooded. Sow bugs (tiny crustaceans) and small spiders are among these adamant groups.

Spiders especially, but also predaceous ants, form a veritable gauntlet that the upward-moving, flood-fleeing invertebrates must run. Because the animals become more concentrated on the tree trunks they make relatively easy prey for the spiders and ants. The spiders and ants, however, also become more vulnerable to other predators, especially birds such as anis, antshrikes, antwrens and antpittas.

Terrestrial mollusks, segmented worms and planarian flatworms are also found on flooded forest tree trunks as they make their way upwards to escape drowning.

Of the insects seen in flooded forests, ants are the most abundant. Many plant species host specific groups of ants. These are the ant-plants and the tree and shrub hosts have apparently evolved structural characteristics that can be turned into a home, or formicarium, by the social insects. Whether these structures arose in direct response to ants is unclear, but today the insects and plants exist in what is probably a mutual relationship. The stinging or biting ants ward off leaf predators, especially other insects, and in some cases their feeding and defecating activity might also help to fertilize the plant species in and on which they live.

Amazonian flooded forest ant-plants are most common in disturbed areas or in habitats recently formed by silt deposition and available for colonization from nearby seed sources. The species that colonize new or disturbed habitats most quickly are those that have their seeds dispersed by animals. No plant group is any faster than the *Cecropia* umbrella or trumpet trees, whose tiny seeds are dispersed by birds, bats, fish and other animals. New alluvial islands or levees will be colonized immediately after the floods and within a year or so it is not uncommon for these habitats to support almost pure stands of *Cecropia* trees.

The *Cecropia* trees are soon colonized by *Azteca* queen ants, which gnaw through the stem to the hollow central cavity. *Cecropia* stems, like bamboo, are divided into compartments. The thin membrane of *Cecropia* stems, however, allows the ant to pass from one chamber to the next. Once the queen has entered a *Cecropia* chamber she then closes the entrance hole with pith material gathered in the hollow stem. The eggs are then laid. The young are fed on secretions furnished by the queen and on pith material. Caretaking of the young is passed on to workers, who also chew holes in the membranes separating the stem chambers so that they can colonize the entire plant. It is at this stage that the workers begin to ward off other colonizing queens and various intruders. The workers feed on peculiar swollen leaf hairs found on the leaves and on special swellings located at the leaf stem. These structures provide oil and carbohydrates. The hairy structures are also used as holdfasts by the ants and greatly increase their stability and mobility on the plants.

Cecropia plants become nearly or totally inundated and the *Azteca* ants move upwards as flood levels rise. It is not uncommon to see only the candelabra-like crown out of water and the huge palmate shaped leaves packed with marooned ants. When this happens, and it does every year, many different insect-eating fish species are attracted to the flooded *Cecropia* trees. When river level has only a few centimetres to rise until the entire plant is submerged, dense balls of ants spend their last few days in huddled hopelessness.

The *tachi*-ants, named after a tree of the family Polygonaceae on which they live, can deliver what is probably the most painful sting of any flooded forest insect. The *tachi*-tree, unlike the *Cecropia* tree, has narrow cavities that split open below each node. This allows easy entrance into the hollow stems for the slim *Pseudomyrmex* ants, or the *tachi*. *Tachi*-tree intruders, including people, can be severely stung by hundreds of these ants which seem to latch almost instantly on to any trespasser. The only redeeming quality of the *tachi*-tree, at least to the local people, is that a concoction made from its bark was traditionally used in folk medicine to treat haemorrhoids.

At the same time as most flooded forest arthropods are scurrying upwards or outwards to escape drowning, aquatic animals begin to colonize the *igapó* from adjacent river channels or floodplain lakes. The animals most easily noticed because of their size and abundance are the fish. The flooded forest is an extremely important spawning habitat for probably the majority of Amazonian fish species. The *igapó* provides both food and cover for young and adult alike. One species that literally follows the floods landward is also one of the most peculiar of Amazonian fish, the arowhana in English or *aruanã* in Amazonian Portuguese. This species is also a prize in the aquarium world, though a difficult fish to keep in confined space.

Arowhanas look as if they have been compressed sideways. They are lithe and smooth swimmers and their wavy movements are somewhat reminiscent of a snake underwater. Their size – up to a metre long – and extremely large and heavily armed mouths suggest predators that feed on other fish. Their rapaciousness, however, is directed much more towards insects than towards fish. Arowhanas, in fact, are probably the largest fish in the world that are principally insect and spider feeders.

Arowhanas are edge species in the sense that they live in or along forests or floating meadows, always on the lookout for insects and spiders falling into the water. They do not stop at insects and spiders, but occasionally are also able to take small birds and bats perched on limbs close to the water. Arowhanas swim gracefully along the water's surface with their chin whiskers (barbels) projected directly forwards in a fashion suggesting that these organs are picking up information about the environment. The exact function of these barbels, however, is still unknown, though in stagnant pools arowhanas appear to use the barbels to rake in the precious little oxygen found where water and air meet. During the breeding season, the barbels also look like young larvae. As discussed later, the barbels are used as a lure to attract the fry back to the male's mouth.

The eye structure of arowhanas explains a lot about their success in locating large quantities of insects and spiders. The arowhana eye is divided by a horizontal partition. The division of the retina into upper and lower parts appears to be an adaptation to deal with markedly dissimilar light levels in and out of water. As arowhanas swim along in search of food, the tops of their large eyes are only a few millimetres below water, at times even projecting slightly out of water. The divided eye allows them to see in and out of water, apparently at the same time. They see falling insects and spiders even before they hit the water, and this certainly gives them an advantage over the large number of other fish that also feed on these invertebrates.

The most peculiar aspect of arowhana feeding behaviour is the ability of the fish to jump out of the water and grab prey off branches, vines and trunks. Amazonian fishermen clearly recognize this jumping ability as they have nicknamed arowhanas 'water-monkeys'. When potential prey has been located on an overhanging piece of vegetation, arowhanas will circle about below and then, at the right moment, compress their bodies into a wave-like spring that, when released, shoots out of the water with such precision that the large mouth just scoops up the victim. Adult arowhanas can jump over a metre out of the water. Large beetles are the most important part of their diet, a reflection perhaps of the abundance of these insects in flooded forests. Birds and bats are probably much more difficult for them to capture, but it is entertaining to watch them try. One case is known where a large arowhana took two recently born sloths. Perhaps the merciless fish jumped out of the water and grabbed the babies from the mother.

As the flood waters rise, the extremely large and opalescent scales turn redder and the male arowhana often, but not always, develops pronounced cheek spots imitating the size and bright pink colour of the female's eggs. Females are attracted to brightly coloured males, as the cheek spots indicate that sperm is ripe. For reasons that are not clear, the right ovary in arowhanas, and its other relatives, has atrophied to the point where it is non-functional so the 150–200 large eggs are confined to the left ovary. Arowhanas are mouth-brooders and it is the male that performs this function. Once the eggs are fertilized, the male grabs them up into the protection of its cavernous mouth. Young arowhanas are born in the father's mouth. The large egg provides the individual larva with an extraordinary yolk-sac. The newborn live off their yolk-sacs for the 2–3 weeks that they remain solely within the male's mouth. Once the yolk-sac has disappeared, and they are about 30–40 millimetres long, the father lets them out of his mouth for feeding sessions on micro-organisms, such as algae, tiny crustaceans and insects. Whenever danger appears, however, the young flee back into the father's mouth and, as mentioned earlier, the large chin barbels appear to orient the young to the mouth. At about 4–6 weeks the young are abandoned to fend for themselves.

In most cases this brooding behaviour is highly efficient for protecting the young. Aquarium trade fishermen, however, use it to their advantage. Fishermen recognize the male by its colours and the slightly swollen cheek pouch between the lower jaw bones. Since arowhanas rest near the surface they can easily be seen. Fishermen attempt to sever the male's head, thus preventing it from swallowing and killing the young, which is usually the case when the fish are captured with a net. As the young flee the decapitated head they are then scooped up with a dip-net and are on their way to Miami, Tokyo or London to adorn someone's aquarium.

In December and January, with rapidly rising water levels, Central Amazonian rivers announce the coming of the new floods. Most of the fish species have just spawned, those that form large schools doing so in the river channels before migrating to the flooded forests. The flooded forest is many things to many different kinds of fish. For a large number of species the *igapó* is a natural orchard where fruits are in abundance. Unlike anywhere else in the world, many fish in the Amazon are highly dependent on fruits and seeds as their main foods. Flooded forest plants bear fruits mostly during the high water period and, of course, this is about the only time that fish have access to these foods.

Of the fruit- and seed-eating fish none is more spectacular than the *tambaqui* (pronounced tam-bah-key), a member of the characin group, to which also belong the piranhas, headstanders and tetras of the aquarium trade. The *tambaqui* reaches over a metre in length and 30 kilogrammes in weight. It is almost always black dorsally but ranges from moss-green to greenish-yellow ventrally – a colour pattern serving to camouflage the fish against a dark bottom and a light surface.

When the *tambaqui* enters flooded forests it swims freely around the trees until it finds its favourite food sources. Though flooded forest trees of the same species can often be found growing grouped together, the more general pattern is that individuals of the same species are scattered about, say each being 50 or more metres from the next adult of its kind.

Looked at head-on, the *tambaqui* appears to have two folding structures on the upper part of its snout a bit like the headlights of a sports car. These structures are nasal flaps which, when raised, increase the flow of water past the olfactory cells in the nose. It is probably through a keen sense of smell that the *tambaqui*, and many other fish as well, are able to locate the tree species on whose fruits and seeds they feed so heavily. Each tree species produces some unique combination of organic compounds, such as latexes, oils, resins and acids that, in effect, are nature's perfumes by which they can be identified. For example, peasants along Amazon rivers refer to the so-called manure-tree – a polite translation for what they actually call it. It is aptly named for it spews stinking odours through the otherwise pleasant redolence of the flooded forest. It is a member of the family Lauraceae to which belong more inviting essences, such as those of bay laurels and cinnamon.

Fish probably have a keener sense of smell in water than humans do in air and, in the dark waters of the *igapó*, olfaction can serve as a guidance system to locate food more easily. Since trees undergo drastic biochemical changes during fruiting periods, it also seems probable that the *tambaqui* and other fruit-eating fish can actually identify, by sense of smell, trees that are dropping their fruits or about to. Of course fish may also smell out fruits that have already dropped into the water, as well as using vision to locate them.

The *tambaqui*'s love of flooded forest fruits is preserved in Amazonian folklore about the jaguar. The sagacious jaguar, it is said, knows in great detail the behaviour of the *tambaqui* for, of all the fish, it is the large cat's favourite when it is in a fish-eating mood. When the floods come, the jaguar works its way along the edge of the inundated forest until it finds a partially submerged rubber tree whose seeds are falling into the water. Once the large feline spots *tambaqui* in the vicinity, it then chooses a horizontal rubber tree branch just off the water's surface to which it swims and on which it perches itself. Spread-eagled on the branch, the jaguar uses the tip of its long tail to beat the water, imitating seeds falling into the water. The *tambaqui* is thus fooled and when it surfaces, mistaking tail for seed, the jaguar rolls off the branch and pounces on the unsuspecting fish. With its sharp claws it grasps the large fish and then hauls the prey ashore for a full meal.

Though the fishing ability of the jaguar is certainly exaggerated in the above tale, Amazonian peasants have traditionally used the same knowledge of the feeding behaviour of the *tambaqui* to catch fish whose favourite food is rubber tree seeds. The peasant fisherman paddles through the flooded forest until he finds a rubber tree dropping its seeds into the water. Below the rubber tree the fisherman then slowly lashes the water with a hookless pole-and-line device to the end of which is attached a large seed. In the other hand a harpoon is made ready. Again, the *tambaqui* is tricked to the surface by the imitation of seeds falling into the water. The fisherman first sees a dark shadow that rises slowly out of the flooded forest understorey. The fish begins to open its mouth very slowly during its ascent and the fisherman sees a flash of large teeth, at which point the harpoon is sent rocketing downwards, breaking the water's surface and continuing until it penetrates its target. Though severely wounded, the extremely strong fish nevertheless takes flight, dislodging the harpoon point from its long shaft. The point is attached to a long line which leads off the shaft. The fisherman abandons the shaft and quickly grabs the line in preparation for a major fight after the fish has been harpooned. A large *tambaqui* will run with the line and has the force to pull the fisherman, still seated in his canoe, all about in the flooded forest until the fish becomes exhausted or the line is entangled around a tree or bush. The catch is then pulled aboard.

When rubber tree seeds are falling into the water the *tambaqui* will eat almost nothing else. There are several species of rubber tree and, though the seeds of all are eaten by some species of fish, Spruce's rubber tree is the one most favoured by the *tambaqui*. It has the largest nuts of all the rubber tree species. Shortly after the floodplains are inundated, rubber tree fruits begin to mature. Their capsules are hard and woody with transverse fibres that are straight when wet but curve in on themselves when dry. This tension causes a sudden explosion under the desiccating force of full sun. Rubber tree capsules mature with the coming of the rainy season, when there are few sunny days. However, what usually happens is that the sun is very hot and intense for a few hours around noon before cloudy skies and rains take over. During the sunny hours, capsules from rubber trees, and other species with exploding capsules, can be heard . . . pop, pop . . . pop, pop, pop . . . pop, pop . . . and so on. Interspersed with the pops are the distinct splashing sounds of fish snapping the seeds off the water's surface. Each fish species has a distinct way of slapping the surface with its tail, thus the skilled fisherman has an acoustical catalogue of sounds in his head for recognizing seed-eating fish even though he cannot see the fish themselves. From the sounds, a fisherman can decide where to go in pursuit of possible catches.

Rubber seeds can be hurled 10–30 metres from the parent tree by the exploding capsules. This produces their initial seed dispersal pattern. The seeds, however, are so heavily sought after by fish and turtles below and birds and monkeys above, that it is amazing any of them escape destruction. The seeds float and hence flooded forest waters move them about. On the other hand, flotation places them at easy reach – the surface – for a long period of time. In flooded forests that are inundated for 5–6 months each year, rubber tree seeds must stay afloat and escape predators for about 2–4 months, that is, until the floodplains are drained and the seeds can come to rest on dry ground. Occasionally seeds may germinate along the shoreline if the water level falls slightly during the floods but, as the floods continue, the plantlets are submerged. The *tambaqui* has no mercy for the newborn and will actually extirpate

Flooded forest and floating meadows are the two main sources of plant energy that fuel life in Amazonian rivers. Two of the most beautiful birds seen along some of these rivers are the blue-backed manakin (top) and the hyacinth macaw (above).

Overleaf: The most curious feature of the Amazon is the flooded forest. Many rainforest tree species have special adaptations to survive long periods of flooding each year.

The Amazon Basin has had a long and complex geological history. Waterfalls (top) in the upper courses of some tributaries mark the presence of ancient sandstones. The Andes (above) are relatively young mountains but are now the source of most of the silt carried by the Amazon River. Geological events have had a profound influence on the distribution of animals within the Amazon Basin. The blue-and-yellow macaw (opposite) is found mostly near rivers, but is missing from many tributary systems.

The Amazon Basin has several different river types. The whitewater rivers, such as the Amazon itself, carry large quantities of silt that give them a muddy colour. Blackwater rivers, such as the Rio Negro, shown here at its meeting with the Amazon River (opposite), are stained by plant compounds. The plant acids that make the Rio Negro dark in colour come from vegetation growing on sandy soils. Sand that is found in the river forms large beaches each year during the low water season (above).

41

The Amazonian rainforest is our planet's most diverse ecosystem. Rivers increase biological diversity in the Amazon because they add an aquatic and amphibious aspect to the rainforest much of which they invade every year with the annual floods.

Overleaf: The flooded forest is the dominant feature of Amazonian floodplains.

Although many flooded forest trees do have buttresses (opposite) – an ideal support where thin soils allow for only a shallow root system – most rainforest trees do not develop them. Many Amazonian birds, such as the toco toucan (top), have evolved to feed on fruits but very few on leaves. The hoatzin (above) is the most highly adapted leaf-eating bird of the Amazon.

When the flooded forest is inundated each year, fish from the river channels and lakes invade it. Amazonian rivers are especially known for their large number of fruit- and seed-eating fish. The tambaqui (top) fattens itself during the floods by eating large quantities of rubber tree seeds and a wide variety of fruits. The flooded forest is also important for river turtles. The big-head (above) is one of the most predatory of Amazonian turtles and bites out large pieces of flesh from its prey in a manner reminiscent of piranhas.

the little plantlet in order to crush the seed that still contains a store of energy.

Ironically, rubber trees, despite the extremely heavy predation on their seeds, are often among the most common trees in flooded forest communities. This piece of evidence indicates that there is not necessarily a correlation between predation and abundance, at least with Amazonian floodplain trees. The most abundant may also be among the species whose seed crops are most heavily destroyed.

Tambaqui teeth are a marvel of dental anatomy. Superficially the fish's dentition, with its huge molars, looks like that of a horse. Of freshwater fish, only the *tambaqui* and some of its South American relatives possess molar-like teeth. Of marine fish, *tambaqui* dentition is reminiscent of the Port Jackson shark, a species that uses its huge blunt teeth to crush mollusks. Interestingly, the fossils of molar-like teeth from fish distantly related to *tambaqui* have been found in East African and Egyptian deposits, a paleontological reminder that Africa, in pre-Ice Age times before tropical forests were greatly reduced by Pleistocene events, was the home to fruit-eating fish as well. Because the Amazon rainforest was much less affected by the Ice Ages, the fruit-eating fish not only survived but even flourished, considering the 200 and more species that now invade the floodplains each year at high water.

Most seeds, unlike those of the rubber tree, probably possess distasteful or poisonous chemicals that help protect them against heavy predation. It is usually thought that, without seed chemical defences which in general would appear to be more potent than structural characteristics of the fruits themselves, the plants would be unable to avoid excessive predation. As the rubber tree seed example illustrates, this is probably only a half truth and many of the distasteful compounds in seeds might simply be the by-product of the plant's chemical make-up, rather than an adaptation *per se* against predators. Seed toxicity is also very relative in the sense that, though poisonous for one group of animals, it might not be at all for another.

Along flooded forest shores large legumes are often the most common seeds found in the driftage. This is in large part because fish ignore them. On the other hand, in areas where large river turtles are still relatively abundant, legume seeds, which are among their favourite food, appear to be much less common.

The floodplain forest and fish interaction is not a one-sided battle of predator attacking seed. Though fish are probably the most important seed predators in Amazonian flooded forests, they are also aquatic vehicles through which many plant species disperse their seeds. Naked seeds with no fleshy material, such as those of rubber trees, are poor candidates for dispersal through animals, as the nut shells are too hard to be digested. If these kinds of seeds were swallowed whole they would be of no nutritional value, and this explains why they are crushed by the fish that eat them. The case is the same with the walnuts we eat. Swallowed whole they cannot be digested. To get an animal to swallow a whole seed an additional attraction, fleshy material, is needed. The fleshy material of fruit has evolved in many different ways. Drupes, berries and special appendages called arils are the most common fleshy fruit arrangements. Fleshy fruit parts serve two principal purposes in flooded forests. First they attract animals that might otherwise not be interested in the plant's seeds because of toxicity factors, and second, they are more often than not buoyancy organs. Fruit buoyancy itself promotes two strategies. The ability to float about in a fleshy raft allows the seeds to be transported far and wide in the flooded forest, thus increasing dispersal distances and potential gene flow from the parent tree. Once the fleshy raft disintegrates, the seeds usually sink to the bottom. Water dispersal alone, however, may be much less important in moving flooded forest seeds about than the fish vehicle. Fleshy fruits floating about in the flooded forest are easily found by fish which then swallow large quantities of them, and thus become sowers of intact seeds. With each defecation seeds are dispersed, and it is also probable that in many cases the ground where they land is also to some extent fertilized by the accompanying faeces. These additional nutrients might favour initial rooting and growth.

Flooded forest seed dispersal through fish is preserved in what is probably an apocryphal but nevertheless entertaining peasant myth. The stone-like and large seeds of many palms can only be eaten by a few fish species. Large catfish swallow them in huge quantities for the outer fleshy covering. The seeds then pass through the intestines to be dispersed in the manner described above. The *tambaqui* fish, endowed with its extremely strong dentition, is able to crush the palm seeds if it wants to. Whole seeds, however, are commonly eaten in large quantities. Amazon folklore explains this behaviour as an adaptation for food storage. Folklore suggests that the large fish swims to the adjacent open waters of lakes or to the river channels where it then defecates the seeds in places they will remain until the low water season. At the end of the floods, that is, after the fruiting season of the flooded forest, the *tambaqui*, it is said, returns to its cache of palm seeds which it now crushes for the rich energy inside the nut wall. This additional energy supposedly further prepares it for low water migrations when almost no food is available in the river channels. This tale probably arose from observations of the *tambaqui* scrounging up old palm seeds at the end of the floods when fresh fruits are no longer available.

By the time the *tambaqui* is forced to leave the *igapó* with the falling water level, it has already added huge fat reserves to its body and head cavities. In fact, over 10 per cent of its weight at the end of the floods consists of fat stores built up from eating large quantities of seeds in the flooded forests. This fat reserve is what it lives on during the low water season when very little other food can be found.

As pointed out earlier, the Amazon flooded forest embraces at least 100 000 square kilometres, a measurement that includes only the surface area of the ground. If the surface area of trunks, branches and leaves is added to the measurement then Amazonian flooded forest, to guess conservatively, embraces a total area in excess of one million square kilometres. With the floods, organic matter floating in the water column becomes attached to trunks, limbs and leaves, to which are also added algae and microscopic animals such as protozoans. There are over 100 fish species that graze on these attached communities, though they do so in several different ways. One group of detritus-feeding fish, called *jaraqui* (jar-a-key), appear to have evolved feeding adaptations that make the flooded forest as important to their life histories as it is for fruit- and seed-eaters.

Jaraqui are characin fish somewhat resembling carp in general form. They are silvery with brightly coloured black and yellow striped tails, and reach about 25–40 centimetres in length. *Jaraqui* have very thick and fleshy lips that can be turned inside out to form a suction pad. The lips are endowed with stubby hair-like teeth that can be used as a rasp and a sieve to remove fine detritus from submerged trees. It appears that the trees themselves release certain organic compounds that enrich the detritus on which the fish feed. Perhaps large numbers of fish defecating in the area of 'detritus-trees' helps to fertilize many plant species in the extremely nutrient-poor waters that bathe them. The tree furnishes some nutrients that the fish might not get in the detritus alone and the tree receives other nutrients though the faeces cycle in greater quantity than could be removed from the water or soil alone.

The selected organic matter on which the *jaraqui* feed is rich in carbohydrates and proteins and, within 2–3 months after entering flooded forest, the fish become very fat. Just after the peak of the floods they begin to form schools and migrate down the tributary rivers. Their exploitation by commercial fishermen is a major seasonal fisheries event in the Central Amazon and is referred to as the 'fat-fish fisheries'.

The easiest way for aquatic animals to escape the draining of the flooded forest is to migrate out of it and into floodplain lakes or to the river channels. Only the larger animals, such as the fish and turtles, are usually seen moving out of the draining forests, but a microscopic investigation would reveal hordes of roundworms, flatworms, segmented worms, minute crustaceans and many types of aquatic insect larvae fleeing to the lakes or channels to pass the low water period. A large part of these animal populations probably does not survive the low water period because of heavy predation and lack of habitat space.

Not all aquatic animals leave the flooded forest when it is drained. Many freshwater bivalve mussels would rather take their chances by staying behind on dry land rather than face a large number of concentrated predators, especially fish and wading birds, in the channels and lakes. Staying behind on dry land, however, means that they cannot feed, since they are filter-feeders that remove plankton and organic matter from the water. The out-of-water phase means they must enter into a quiescent state in which their developmental and metabolic processes are slowed down to save enough body energy to survive on dry land for several months. Interestingly, this quiescent state appears to be driven by internal processes rather than external factors (lack of water). Even when water, and hence food, are still available towards the end of the floods, the mussels already begin a period of growth stagnation. Behaviourally and physiologically it is as if two months or so have been added to the beginning of the average dry phase of the flooded forest. So why does a mussel waste two months doing little if anything to promote its growth?

Man has only been recording Amazon flood levels accurately since the beginning of this century. Mussels and other animals have been doing it, behaviourally and genetically, since each became its own species with its special adaptations. The flooding times in most years are pretty much the same and thus animals have a fairly predictable average to go by. It is the odd year that is of greatest ecological concern. At least twice in this century Amazonian flooded forests, due to exceedingly low flood levels, were subjected to dry phases 2–3 months longer than normal. We already know that the Amazon Basin has gone through relatively long periods much drier than at present. The occasional dry year is perhaps a climatic reminder of earlier periods. Genetically, mussels still 'remember' these dry periods and that is perhaps why they prepare themselves for them in what appears to be a 2–3 month safety period.

The production of two generations during the floods is also an adaptation to help ensure mussel survival. The dry-phase mussels, or first generation, suffer about 98 per cent mortality. The survival of the species depends on the remaining 2 per cent which, however, are sufficient to produce a large second generation that suffers relatively little mortality in the flooded forest. The second generation, of course, subsequent to the passing of the floods and the onset of the dry phase, becomes the first generation in the continuing life cycle.

Flooded forest filter-feeders are diverse in kind and shape, but none are more varied than sponges. The great majority of sponges are marine but one family has managed to colonize freshwater and is well represented on the trees in Amazonian flooded forests. Freshwater sponges face quite different challenges to those of their marine relatives. Those in the Amazonian *igapó* forests are found on trees that are seasonally inundated. Most flooded forest sponge colonies are relatively small, usually about the size of a tennis ball. Their size is perhaps limited by the long periods they must remain dormant when the waters recede. The internal network of the sponge is made up of a maze of interconnected and branching spaces, channels and chambers. Special filaments produce currents that pass through the sponge's chambers where bacteria and organic detritus are captured. Sponges must also obtain relatively large amounts of silicon for the formation of spicules – the basic building blocks of their structure – and a lack of this this mineral, along with seasonal desiccation, limits their populations in flooded forests.

When river levels fall, sponges are left hanging on the tree trunks and branches like Christmas decorations. Before this happens, however, they produce an ingenious life-preserving package, a gemmule, in which the necessary genetic information and reproductive cells are sealed. The gemmule is a very tiny spherical structure, hardened on the outside by a secreted layer covered by spicules, and this case protects the live cells within. When the waters return the gemmules germinate and initiate growth. The gemmule also serves as a dispersal unit because water can transport it about until it lands where it can to begin its growth. Old sponges, however, retain many if not most of their gemmules and these germinate on the dead structure of previous years.

Several arthropod groups also anticipate the draining of the flooded forest with large numbers of individuals descending the tree trunks as water level falls. Spiders, pseudo-scorpions and other arachnids, along with centipedes, may start their descents 4–6 weeks before the waters recede from the lower trunk area. Much of this early descent, especially by the large numbers of spiders observed, appears to be a type of troop displacement in order to ambush other arthropods, such as beetles and ants, that will subsequently move downwards to the forest floor when it is drained.

Many of the arthropods that colonize the forest floor during the dry period appear to breed there in order to place their young in a habitat of food abundance. Spiders are among the first to breed on the drained ground and their juveniles can become very common. As the dry season progresses, flies and beetles become more abundant on the forest floor. On the tree trunks winged insects, such as cockroaches, bugs, crickets, moths and beetles, tend to dominate. Ants, however, become the most active and ubiquitous migrants, moving between canopy, trunk region and forest floor in search of food.

CHAPTER THREE

FLIGHT
IN THE
FOREST

L ife above floodwater is not very different, in terms of the basic adaptations needed to live in trees, to life above dry ground for arboreal animals. The flooded and upland forest canopies are interconnected, though from the air one can always distinguish them by their slightly different green colours and the drop in elevation of the floodplains which gives the impression that the *igapó* forest is lower than its non-flooded counterpart. In general, the flooded forest loses a few metres of stature compared to adjacent upland rainforest, and it also falls behind in its diversity of tree species. Reduced plant diversity seems to lead to fewer species of insects and other invertebrates in the canopy, but to what extent is not yet known because of the great difficulty of sampling this habitat. It should be remembered, however, that the invertebrate fauna of the *igapó* is still very diverse compared to, say, a forest in the temperate latitudes. At present we do not know the life history of even one invertebrate species in the flooded forest canopy, and indeed these treetops are one of the most unexplored major tropical habitats.

Canopy vertebrate animals are much better known because they are larger and considerably easier to observe. No major arboreal group of vertebrate animals found in upland forest is missing from the *igapó*. The interconnected canopies allow easy travel between the two forest types, though there are many species that avoid one habitat type or the other. When this is the case, there are often different but very similar species living in each habitat type.

Birds are by far the most diverse group of vertebrates in flooded forest canopies. An average hectare of tall *igapó* can be visited by as many as 150 bird species in the course of a year. Mammalian diversity in an average hectare rarely exceeds 50 species, bats accounting for about half of that total, whereas amphib-

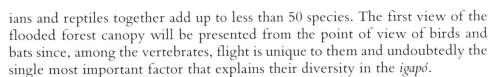

ians and reptiles together add up to less than 50 species. The first view of the flooded forest canopy will be presented from the point of view of birds and bats since, among the vertebrates, flight is unique to them and undoubtedly the single most important factor that explains their diversity in the *igapó*.

South America easily qualifies as the 'bird continent'. It claims about one-third of the world's bird species for itself but is the only continent where songbirds are in a minority. About 900, or one-tenth, of all the bird species on the planet are found in the Amazon Basin, and a little less than half of these are endemic – that is, found only there and nowhere else. Ornithologists who have turned their binoculars on the Ice Ages, and even further back in time, believe that the diversity of the Amazonian bird fauna is due in large part to the fragmentation of the rainforest when drier climates prevailed. Arboreal birds were supposedly forced into forest refuges that were geographically isolated from one another. These refuges in turn led to genetic isolation and the origin of new species. With wetter conditions, as at present, the rainforest once again became the dominant vegetation and the refuge birds, in large part, dispersed from their centres of origin.

What role did flooded and riparian (river-bank) forests have in shaping the Amazon bird fauna? One hectare of undisturbed Amazonian flooded forest is used by an average of about 125 bird species, though all will not be present in any given area at the same time. The bird diversity found in flooded forest per given area is quite comparable to that of the adjacent upland. This of course leads to the conclusion that seasonal or daily flooding, the latter in the tidal forests of the Lower Amazon, has no effect on bird diversity in comparison to non-flooded areas. In fact, bird diversity in flooded forests is largely a reflection of that found on the nearby upland, since most of the species are the same. Many species, however, will be more dominant in one of the habitats than the other. Subtraction, especially of ground-dwelling birds, rather than the addition of unique species, is the rule for *igapó* birds. There are very few bird species restricted only to Amazonian flooded forests.

The rainforest, in many ways, is like a multi-storey business building where distinct groups of activities are concentrated on different floors, or tiers of floors, with many workers moving from one level to the next during the course of a day or night. The vertical division of the rainforest is shown most clearly with birds because of their diversity and, of course, the conquest of the vertical dimension by flight. Most birds will tend to favour only one or two of the four main recognizable levels of the rainforest – ground, lower, middle and upper tiers. Very few species move freely about in all four levels though, where forests are low in stature, the upper three divisions may be reduced to two and the vertical zonation of birds is more difficult to establish.

Though flooding does not necessarily decrease bird diversity, it neverthe-

 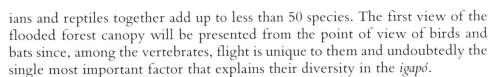

less has a far-reaching effect on the *igapó* avian communities. With the floods the ground level and lower and middle canopies are inundated, thus causing birds normally restricted to these habitats either to migrate to upland forest or to be concentrated in the upper levels. Both responses can be observed, though most bird species appear to choose either one or the other.

Flooding, of course, has the most challenging effect on ground birds and one might expect them to be largely absent from flooded forests, even during the non-flooding season, especially as this is when fruits and seeds are scarce. The ground bird fauna of rainforests in general is poor compared to its counterparts in grassland and shrub areas. Gallinaceous birds (Galliformes), to which belong the familiar chickens, turkeys and quail, are in general the most successful ground dwellers of the avian world. As we will see shortly, the gallinaceous birds that have been most successful in South American rainforests, including flooded forests, have largely taken to the trees.

In the flooded forest, tinamous, which are grouse-like birds, replace the gallinaceous species and colonize the floodplains each year when the water level falls. The flooded forests on river islands, however, are inaccessible since tinamous do not retreat or colonize through flight. They literally follow the receding floods riverward, during a 4-6 month period each year, at the same time feeding on fallen fruits and seeds left behind by the floods or eating small invertebrates that are also recolonizing the forest floor.

A few of the tinamous species also nest on the floodplains. Their nests are generally found in holes, which they cover with leaves, near tree trunks. Tinamous are poor fliers and normally only take to the wing as a last recourse. Poor flight and a terrestrial existence versus a large number of potential predators, ranging from cats to snakes, requires an additional adaptation – camouflage. Tinamous, in fact, can often be heard a few metres away but not seen because of their excellent hiding abilities. Their melodious flute-like whistles often seem to be produced by a bush, until closer inspection reveals the ground bird. Humans are the greatest garbage producers on earth, and tinamous are fond of 'hanging out' on the periphery of campsites or small villages. Unfortunately for them, they are considered fine game birds and are certainly among the most commonly killed birds every year in floodplain areas adjacent to upland. Tinamous are part of the so-called backyard fauna of Amazon peasants and are one of the birds on their way to incipient domestication, as they keep well and can put up with people who do not shoot at them.

The hoatzin and umbrellabird are perhaps the Amazonian flooded forest's greatest gifts plucked from the avian world. As explained earlier, most of the other birds found in flooded forests are either widely distributed both in and outside the Amazon or found also on upland. The hoatzin and umbrellabird are so closely associated with flooded forests or the river's edge that it seems reason-

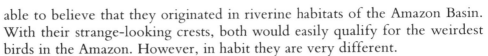

able to believe that they originated in riverine habitats of the Amazon Basin. With their strange-looking crests, both would easily qualify for the weirdest birds in the Amazon. However, in habit they are very different.

The first thing that strikes one about the umbrellabird is that it appears to have been the model for the traditional Amazonian Indian haircut. It ranges in colour from black to glossy blue. Its crest is formed of feathers that are very thickly set with hairy plumes curving over at the end. The crest can be 5–8 centimetres high in males and projects as far forward as the end of the beak. When the crest is erected – it can also be laid back so as to be hardly visible – it is reminiscent of a panache worn on the helmet of a royal court guard. Of Amazonian birds, only the Guianan cock-of-the-rock rivals the umbrellabird in crest development. The umbrellabird goes one step further, however – males have an additional ornamental appendage that hangs from the lower throat region in the form of a long wattle covered in front by shiny blue feathers. The wattle can be pressed against the body so it is nearly invisible, or it can be erected to conceal the forepart of the body. The crest and wattle are used in sexual displays.

The umbrellabird is not commonly found in upland forests. It prefers the tops of floodplain and river island trees, and it is usually very difficult to observe. It also seems probable that since the advent of commercialized rubber collecting, which has traditionally been concentrated in floodplain and riverine island habitats, umbrellabird populations have diminished because they have been a target of subsistence hunting. For example, Alfred Russel Wallace, the great nineteenth-century naturalist, described umbrellabirds as being 'tolerably abundant' during his travels in the Central Amazon region near Manaus, but such is not the case today. Not only hunting but floodplain deforestation as well have reduced umbrellabird populations in this area. One's best chance of seeing an umbrellabird is when it crosses rivers, as it often does in search of fruit trees. It feeds on fleshy fruits and large insects found in the tops of trees. It also nests in the tops of trees but little is known about its reproductive behaviour.

The hoatzin, certainly the Amazonian flooded forest's most peculiar bird, is an enigma in many ways. It is the only species in its family, and its relationship to other bird families remains a mystery. It is confined to flooded and mangrove forests in the Amazon, Orinoco and Guianas. The hoatzin is about the size of a chicken and adorned with a bright blue face and a fan-shaped, almost 'spike-like' crest that would make it a strong contestant in a punk hairdo contest.

The hoatzin is not the Boeing of the bird world. In fact, watching its heavy and loud, but always short, flights makes one want to cheer it on in fear that it might not make its target. Most of the hoatzin's flight time is logged when travelling the short distances between the taller forest where it roosts and the arum or umbrella tree patches where it feeds, usually during the day. No other bird in Amazonian flooded forests is so highly adapted to feed on leaves as the hoatzin.

Unlike any other bird the hoatzin has a double crop – sac-like enlargements in or near a bird's gullet where food is stored before digestion – that exceeds 10 per cent of its weight. The large quantity of leaves usually fermenting in the crops is responsible for the fetid smell associated with hoatzins, or stink-birds, as they are sometimes called.

In flooded forest, hoatzins are often found near arum patches. Arums are herbaceous plants, but some can grow up to 5 metres in height. They have thick stalks, huge leaves and a spreading root system. They are most common in mud-flats beside the forests or in flooded areas that are inundated for too long a period for woody trees to survive. They anchor themselves to the bottom by their spreading root systems but, if flooding becomes too deep, rising water level extirpates them from the bottom and the entire community begins to float. The root system of the arum community becomes an interlocking network that provides a substrate for many other plants, such as sedges, and for animal life.

Hoatzins nest in flooded forest trees during the high water period, and usually no more than a few hundred metres from where they feed. The hoatzin nest is not a thing of beauty and its architectural design is about as simple as one can imagine nidification to be. The nest consists of a crude platform built of twigs and it is usually placed on a branch over water. Several nests are often found in the same tree or relatively close to each other. Two or three eggs are laid, and they must be incubated for about three weeks to a month. The eggs, which often go unattended when the birds are feeding, are highly vulnerable and are heavily preyed on by monkeys, snakes and birds. Hoatzins that lose their eggs lay again, but often in a different nest. The young are fed fermented leaves from the adult's crop. Hoatzins usually fly about in pairs joined together to form small bands. During the reproduction period, however, it is not uncommon to see three adults attending the same nest.

Young hoatzins are undoubtedly among the most peculiar of birds. Unlike any other species, the young have a pair of claws on each wing. Even more strangely these claws are not at the end but rather at the bend of the wing. It is unclear whether this clawed condition represents primitive anatomy or an adaptation that was and still is peculiar to the hoatzins. Wing claws were also possessed by *Archaeopteryx*, the famous Jurassic bird so well known from fossils, but they were anatomically quite different from those of hoatzins. Young hoatzins use their claws to clamber about on, and hang from, branches. When confronted with danger, the young birds drop into the water to flee potential predators. Of course, in the water the chicks are vulnerable to predatory fish, and perhaps caimans and some snakes, and for that reason they attempt to reach a tree or bush as soon as possible. With the help of their wing claws, they pull themselves back up to their nests when danger has passed to await their parents returning with a crop of leaves. With the appearance of permanent plumage and ability to fly, the young hoatzins lose their wing claws. The adult birds fly away from danger, instead of 'falling' away from it as do the young.

South America might also be called the 'fruit continent'. Its forests, especially the rainforests, have the most diverse range of fruits and likewise frugivorous animals, of any continental region. Of the vertebrate animals, birds claim the highest diversity of fruit-eating species. The main fruit-eating birds of Amazonian flooded forests are the macaws, parrots, parakeets, currasows, toucans, cotingas and its relatives, manakins, oropendolas, some finches and tanagers. This fruit-eating group certainly contains the majority of the most beautiful birds found in flooded forests.

A distinction needs to be made between seed-eaters and fruit-eaters. Seed-eaters are interested in the seed component of the fruit, whereas fruit-eaters are after the pulp or other fleshy material and, in some cases, the seeds as well. In general seed-eaters prefer dry fruits, that is, devoid of any pulp that might take work to remove. Furthermore, for hard seeds to be digested they first need to be cracked before swallowed, otherwise they pass intact through the animal. Very few animals in the Amazonian flooded forest can deal with large seeds. Many animals, however, can eat pulp and other fleshy fruit material, regardless of the size of the seeds it surrounds. Small-seeded dry fruits are in the minority in Amazonian flooded forests. In general seed-eating by small birds is much more common in open habitats, such as meadows and grasslands, than in the forest communities. Finches, for example, are a diverse seed-eating group found mostly in open habitats. However, they tend to become much more fruit-eating when inhabiting the Amazonian flooded forests.

The gallinaceous birds that have been successful in Amazonian rainforest have moved upwards, that is, into the trees. Nevertheless, to some extent it appears that they all retain an atavistic ability to forage on the ground. The currasows are the most common gallinaceous birds in the Amazonian *igapó*. They are attracted to the floodplains during the inundation period when fruit is in plentiful supply. The razor-billed currasow fills its crop and intestinal system with up to perhaps 15–20 per cent of its own weight in succulent fruits. It feeds high in the trees of the flooded forest. Though in upland forest currasows will descend to the ground to take fallen fruit, in flooded forest they do not attempt to feed on the fallen fruit floating on the water's surface. During the low water period floodplain populations migrate to the upland forests. In drier parts of the Amazon Basin their loud chattering can often be heard in the morning hours when they move to the river or stream edge to take water. Currasows are probably the finest game birds in the Amazon and it is likely that Man is the major predator on adult populations. Their chattering, which betrays their presence, is often answered by the report of a hunter's shotgun.

To eat and sleep in the same place can be dangerous for an animal because it increases the chances of predators locating it. Amazonian macaws and parrots avoid this problem by flying to feeding sites each morning and then returning to sleeping habitats in the late afternoon. Flooded forests in the Amazon play a double role in the ecology of macaws and parrots. Firstly, wherever possible, Amazonian macaws and parrots will return to flooded or river edge forest to roost. They also seem to choose feeding and roosting sites on opposite sides of a river. In the early morning, flying so closely together that they seem to be one bird with four wings, pairs are seen and heard crossing rivers to reach their feeding sites. Often the macaw and parrot traffic can be two-way as flocks commuting from opposite banks pass each other in flight.

The second important role of flooded forests to macaws and parrots is one of nutrition. They prefer seeds to pulp and are in many cases major seed-predators in flooded forests. They are able to get at seeds encased in tough capsules by holding them down with their feet and breaking them open with their strong beaks. Macaws and parrots seem to be especially fond of euphorb seeds and palm fruits, both of which are generally high in protein and carbohydrates. In the Amazon they often feed on the fruits or seeds of so-called species pairs, that is, one species restricted to flooded forest and its pair to upland forest. This is necessary because flooded and upland forest require different adaptations and so there are relatively few tree species that do well in both habitats. There are many plant groups, however, where closely related species have evolved so that one can tolerate flooding whereas the other is restricted to upland forest. Some of the spiny palms are a good example of this. The flooded species produce fruit crops for a 2 month period subsequent to the main flood peak. Their upland counterparts, however, are in fruit somewhat later. By using both the flooded and upland forests, the macaws have access to the fruits of at least two different species of each of the spiny palm groups. However, from the birds' nutritional point of view the species of each of the palm pairs produce the same type of fruit and, even better, it is available for a much longer period than if production from only one forest type were available.

During the low water period macaws and parrots are occasionally seen in large flocks on the ground along river banks or cliffs. In some cases they land in these areas in search of pebbles which they need for grinding and digesting their food. They also eat mineralized earth, apparently for the salts contained therein.

Macaws and large parrots do not appear to use most flooded forests for nesting to any great extent, though many parakeets do. All of the larger species nest in the hollows of trees. There may be a shortage of these habitats in flooded forest, considering that rodents, snakes and many other bird species also live or nest in holes. Macaws and the larger parrots, however, nest in tall trees, and perhaps the fact that the upland forest is higher in stature is the main factor that attracts them there rather than a lack of nesting holes.

Naturalists often use the ideas expressed in native folklore as hypotheses for scientific experiments. Take, for example, the strangely yellow-coloured macaws and parrots traditionally kept by many of the native Amerindian tribes in the Amazon and elsewhere in Brazil. Ornithologists have known for many decades that the yellowness of many captive macaws and parrots was an aberrant condition, though it could not be determined what factors were responsible for the colouring. Amerindians had less doubt about it, as they invariably claimed credit for the biological engineering of yellow feathers through the application of unguents or by force-feeding the birds special substances. These ointments and substances, fed to the birds supposedly to colour their feathers yellow, are made variously from frog blood, turtle eggs or fish fat. The application, either external or internal, of these substances usually takes place after the bird's feathers have been pulled out.

The colouration of a bird's feather is due either to chemical or physical colours or to a combination of both. Chemical colours are produced by certain compounds (carotenoids) that are diffused in the feathers, and these produce the yellows, oranges and various reds. Physical colours, on the other hand, are derived from the reflection of light by the micro-structure of the feather which is impregnated with melanin. This produces the blues and the metallic and iridescent sheens that make the macaws and parrots such beautiful birds. The colour of the hyacinth macaw, for example, is due solely to physical colours. A lack of melanin in the feathers of hyacinth macaws produces albinos. However, a lack of melanin in the multi-coloured macaws and parrots results in the greater diffusion of the yellow-producing compounds by the chemical colouring process. Thus the artificially induced-yellow macaws and parrots are, in a sense, albinos, although the condition can apparently be reversed. Recent evidence shows that the yellowness is due to physiological reactions causing an arrest in melanin production as a result of the trauma the birds suffer when their feathers are pulled out. So it seems that the strangely beautiful induced-yellow macaws and parrots of Brazil are produced by torture rather than tincture. The Amerindians got this one wrong in their folklore.

A body built to fly a beak seems like a fair description of toucan anatomy. No Amazonian forest birds have gone as far as the toucans in the evolution of long and large beaks, not to mention very colourful as well. In at least two of the species the beak in adults can be longer than the bird's body. A toucan's beak, however, is not the heavy third hand it appears to be but rather a quite light structure supported internally by a spongy web of bony struts and tissue. The edge of the beak is sharp with teeth-like protuberances, a feature that renders it both a food and protection tool. Size alone would be enough to call attention to a toucan's beak but evolution has gone even further, in most species, by decorating this appendage with outlandish colours. Even more peculiar, in some of the species the inside of the beak is also highly coloured. Ornithologists feel that the bright colouring of toucans' beaks acts as a signal to ward off predators and other aggressive animals. The beak's colours say, 'get too close and you will be bitten'.

Toucans can often be seen crossing rivers in a manner similar to that described for macaws and parrots above, though much more irregularly. Unlike macaws and parrots, however, their movements consist of a series of wing beatings followed by planing.

Toucans feed mainly on fleshy fruits, some of which are enveloped in capsules requiring strong beaks to break them open. Of the large fruit-eating birds, toucans differ considerably in behaviour from the currasows, macaws and parrots. Currasows eat fleshy fruits and ingest their seeds as well. Macaws and parrots are interested mostly in seeds. Toucans might well be called seed-spitters. Unlike the other large fruit-eating birds of Amazonian flooded forests, toucans tend to avoid swallowing seeds. Of course, tiny seeds, such as those of figs, cannot easily be separated from the fruit flesh, and thus must be ingested. Toucans are most common in flooded forests during the floods when fruit is most abundant. They undoubtedly play an important role as seed dispersal agents for many plant species. Little nesting appears to take place in the *igapó*, but rather in the upland forests where they use holes in the higher trees.

Most birds build their nests in relatively hidden or hard to get at places to avoid predation on their eggs and young. Caciques and oropendolas appear to do just the opposite. The large colonies of woven, pouch-like nests of yellow-rumped and red-rumped caciques are common sights in the trees of Amazonian flooded forests. Cacique colonies of several dozen individual nests are often seen hanging over the water at the river's edge. In some cases, during the floods when rivers can be 10–12 metres higher than in the low water period, cacique nests are occasionally found hanging only a few metres above the river. Oropendolas tend to build their nests in higher trees, and river islands, where tall forest remains, are favoured as roosting sites. The crested and green oropendolas are often seen in huge flocks crossing river channels in their daily movements to and from islands. Superficially, cacique and oropendola nests with their eggs and young look highly vulnerable to attack by predators. Closer inspection, however, will almost always reveal wasp, bee or ant nests nearby. The proximity of stinging or biting social insects acts as a deterrent to potential predators.

Caciques and oropendolas rival macaws and parrots as the noisiest birds found along Amazonian rivers. Camping near a yellow-rumped or red-rumped cacique colony is unlike any other experience. On the negative side it can be earsplitting and obnoxious to the point that one is forced to move to a new site. It can also be a pleasing experience, as caciques are able to imitate the sounds and calls of other birds and a variety of mammals, thus giving the impression that an acoustical menagerie is nearby. Colonies near peasant farms even take to imitating fowl and other domestic animals.

Caciques and oropendolas are able to use their sharp, pointed beaks as both pincers and borers. Their boring technique is unique. The beak is first employed in a closed position to puncture soft vegetable matter, such as fruit pulp, rotten wood and rolled-up leaf shoots. Once the bore is established, it is widened by opening the beak while it is still inside. These bore holes allow the birds to see what is inside, such as pulp, juice or insects, which they then extract with their beaks. Caciques and oropendolas live on a mixed diet, but during the floods fleshy fruits are their most important food in flooded forests.

Cacique and oropendola colonies usually nest in only one tree and often only on one large branch. Their singing – mostly performed by the males – is accompanied by contortions and often much wing beating which adds to the overall musical effect. Though the males make the most noise, females seem to do the most work as it is left to them to construct the nests and care for the young. Males are larger but much fewer in number, and polygamy is probably common.

The polygamous habit is associated with the fruit-eating cotingas and manakins as well. Perhaps an abundance of fruit is the principal reason why the female is able to raise the young alone. The cotingas are among the most beautiful of the small birds to visit flooded forest during the fruiting season. They tend to spend most of their time in the higher parts of the canopy but swoop down to lower levels to take drupes and berries which they carry off to a perch. Berries are swallowed whole, but they spit out the larger seeds of drupes. These small birds feed on many of the same fruits that bats do, including figs, the long catkins of umbrella trees and a large number of mistletoes. The seeds of epiphytes or hemi-parasites, such as the figs and mistletoes, are heavily dispersed by these small birds because they tend to defecate in a different place to where they obtain their fruit.

Of the smaller birds found in flooded forests, the manakins have the most elaborate dances and displays. In upland forests the manakins usually descend to near the forest floor where females sit quietly while males go through various dances and displays – repertoires include jumping, vibrating, cowering and elaborate movements of the wings. In upland some of the manakin species clear small areas on the forest floor that are repeatedly used as courting arenas where the periodic sexual displays by males take place. In the *igapó*, seasonal flooding appears to preclude the establishment of annually visited courting arenas, so manakin displays are confined mostly to lower branches, vines or fallen logs. Most of the manakin species found in upland forest probably enter the *igapó* to some extent to feed on fruits when they are abundant during the flooding period. Only two or three manakin species, however, nest in flooded forest.

The dance of the crimson-headed manakin involves two males jumping back and forth between adjacent branches, whilst making sharp clicking sounds. Alternatively, the birds vibrate their bodies and display by sliding from side to side on a low perch. Blue-backed manakin dances, preceded by a series of sonorous introductions, consist of two males jumping repeatedly and in turn in an arc over the rival's back. Once females are attracted, a male will then fly silently about one of them, landing at short intervals, until realizing the sexual act.

Manakins have played a heavy part in Amazonian superstition and folklore. They are considered as mascots, unfortunately for them dead and dried, instead of alive. Used as a talisman, some manakin species were traditionally buried at the entrances of shops or grog-shops to improve business and health.

Certainly among the most beautiful birds of the Amazonian rainforest are the male trogons with their resplendent metallic greens and blues and red or yellow stomach. Females are more drab, as with many bird species. The white-tailed, black-tailed and violaceous trogons are the only species of their group that regularly enter the flooded forests of the Central Amazon. Trogons for the most part are solitary birds. Like the cotingas they do not perch to take fruits, but rather pluck them while in flight and carry them elsewhere to be eaten. Again, this is good seed-dispersal behaviour. Other than fruits, trogons also feed on flying insects, which they take on the wing. They also take a variety of ground invertebrates along the flooded forest's edge.

Trogons do not build nests *per se*, but excavate holes in abandoned tree termitaria. Termite nests are shared with other birds as well, such as some parakeets. Females and males take turns incubating the 2–4 eggs. Trogon homes in termite nests can become fetid chambers in the few weeks that the young inhabit them. Faeces and other organic material build up providing an egg-laying habitat for flies. Maggots flourish in trogon waste.

As mentioned earlier, most plants in tropical rainforest are pollinated by animals with wind playing only a secondary role in the community as a whole. Though animal pollination is clearly recognized as one of the biological foundations on which the rainforest stands, it has been little studied. No one knows for sure which animals pollinate most of the species, though flower structure and colour are often strong clues. 'Bird flowers', for example, tend to have cup-shaped flowers and they are often red. Many types of birds feed on nectar but most of them, other than the hummingbirds, tend to turn to this food only when fruits and insects are not easily available. In the avian world, hummingbirds are the guardian angels of flower nectar.

Hummingbirds are a very large avian group restricted to the New World. One would expect their greatest diversity to be in the Amazon Basin because there are more flowering plant species there than in any other region of the world. Mountain valleys, however, such as those found in the Colombian and

Ecuadorian Andes, have favoured the evolution of more hummingbird species than the lowland tropical rainforest. Nevertheless, the Amazonian hummingbird fauna is still diverse. Around the port city of Belém, which is south of the Amazon River mouth, over 20 hummingbird species can be found and about half of these enter flooded forest.

Four or five hummingbird species are commonly found in the same general area of flooded forest, but many more than that are visitors during the flowering season. Hummingbirds are among the most habitat tolerant birds in the sense that the same species have home ranges, at least seasonally, embracing several types of flooded and upland forests. The abundance of flowers, rather than forest type, is the factor that controls their presence in any given area. Flooded forest plants begin to flower just after the peak of the floods, that is, with the cessation of heavy rains and the beginning of the dry season. In most flooded forests, then, flowering appears to begin about 2–3 months before these communities are drained with falling river levels. Flowers are common in Amazonian flooded forests for about 6–8 months each year, whereas fruits are abundant for only about six months. There is also peak-flowering during the dry season in Amazonian upland forest, and one wonders if there is competition between the two communities for hummingbird and other animal pollinators. Also, it is not at all clear whether flowers are in sufficient quantity all the year round for nectar-feeders. During periods of few flowers – especially during the heavy rains – hummingbirds are forced to turn to insects, spiders and other invertebrates.

Hummingbirds prefer tropical forest nectars of relatively low sugar concentrations, for example, about 20 per cent as compared to double that in the flowers exploited by bees. Considering the high metabolic rate of hummingbirds – some can eat nearly their own weight in nectar per day – this may seem a paradox. Diluted nectar, however, flows more easily than a thicker solution through the narrow beak-pump of hummingbirds, and pretty much the same is true of nectar-feeding bats and sphingid moths. Also, hummingbirds, bats and sphingid moths treat flowers like fast-food joints, as they like to get in and out in as brief a time as possible. A more viscous solution might detract them, thus the flower would lose its pollinator.

Birds of prey are by far the most successful as well as the main predators on vertebrates in the flooded forest canopy. Most of the raptorial (predatory) birds, however, also feed on various invertebrates, some even more than on vertebrate animals. Raptors use two different hunting techniques, though each species normally only practises one of these. The first method of hunting involves taking prey while the predator is on the wing. Alternatively, the raptor can perch on a limb and fall on its prey below. This method is most effective when there is dry ground below as the prey can be imprisoned against it with the talons. This type of hunting in flooded forest is limited because water eliminates ground-dwelling prey and only the specialized species can catch fish. Nevertheless, the tree trunks and stems can be used as a base for finding and holding prey until it can be carried away or eaten on the spot. The fish-eating raptors hunt mostly in open habitats, such as floodplain lakes and river channels.

The largest bird to visit Amazonian flooded forest is the harpy eagle. It is also one of the largest and mightiest eagles in the world, females standing almost a metre in height with a wing span reaching nearly 2 metres. Males are substantially smaller. This enormous raptor has extremely large and strong legs, and talons with long claws. It perches on the tops of tall trees but descends into the lower levels of the forest where it can pursue its prey through branches and around other obstacles with great agility. It feeds on sloths, monkeys, porcupines, currasows, macaws and other large prey which it often carries to the tops of tall trees before ripping it to pieces. The harpy eagle constructs its bulky nest on the highest branches of the tallest trees, though now probably only very rarely in flooded forest due to hunting pressure. Peasant hunters consider it one of the most prestigious species that can be killed, not really for food, but for macho enhancement.

Of the giant raptors the black hawk-eagle is probably the commonest to appear in flooded forests. Amazonians call it the monkey-hawk because it feeds so heavily on primates in the rainforest. It can swoop down along the edge of the forest and grab a monkey by the head with its huge talons and then carry the primate, jerking and tremoring in its flight of death, to a high branch where it is eaten.

One of the most interesting and aberrant birds of prey within the flooded forest is the crane-hawk. Unlike most raptors this species clambers along branches in search of its broad array of prey. It has extremely long legs, so long in fact that they pass the tail when the bird is flying. A very flexible joint at the end of the toes gives the claws great mobility to inspect the insides of tree holes for frogs, lizards, cockroaches and bats. The crane-hawk is also able to probe into bromeliads by spreading the leaves with its feet.

Owls are seldom seen in flooded forests because they are nocturnal and their excellent camouflaging, combined with hiding in tree holes by day, make them difficult to find. At night, however, they are commonly heard and assume the predatory roles of many of the diurnal (daytime) raptors. The two commonest species encountered are the great horned owl and the spectacled owl. They feed on small mammals, reptiles, amphibians and large insects. Barn owls are probably becoming more common in many floodplain areas where deforestation had led to the more open habitats. This species, which is nearly world-wide in distribution, does not enter dense forest. It is most commonly seen and heard near floodplain villages and towns, perhaps because of an abundance of rodents and other prey associated with human settlement. Owls, unlike raptors, do not digest feathers, hair, scales and bones, but rather regurgitate them after the prey flesh has been dissolved by gastric acids in the intestinal tract. This regurgitated material, found in or beneath their roosting holes, serves as a dietary signpost to their feeding behaviour.

Unless one looked very carefully during the day, or investigated the night hours, the Amazonian flooded forest's most diverse mammal group, the bats, could largely be missed. Floodplain forests provide excellent roosting and feeding sites for bats, all of which are solely nocturnal. Bats, of course, are the only mammals that can fly any distance but not the only ones that navigate by echo-location. Echo-location has evolved independently several times in the animal kingdom, and in the Amazon the bats and dolphins use this kind of navigation. Echo-location in bats operates by the production of sounds, usually ultra-sonic, that when bounced off objects produce patterns recognizable as specific items, including prey. Bats have large and highly modified ears that act as enhanced sound collectors to gather wavelength signals and send them on to the brain for object interpretation.

Vampire bats are one of the feared animals of Amazonian floodplains. However, their danger to Man is little, if any, from a practical point of view. Humans who sleep outside are occasionally bitten, but reported enervation is more likely to be due to undetected malaria than to vampire bats. It is highly likely that Man has inadvertently helped increase vampire bat populations along Amazonian rivers by the introduction of livestock. Livestock, especially cattle, provide excellent hosts for the blood-feeding vampires.

Unfortunately, little is known about the blood hosts vampire bats used before the introduction of cattle. During the flooding season most ground mammals, such as tapirs and peccaries, retreat to higher ground, thus they are not available as blood sources. The extent to which vampire bats might feed on arboreal animals is largely unknown.

Contrary to popular myth, vampire bats do not suck blood. The host's skin is punctured by razor-sharp incisor teeth and anti-coagulant saliva is injected into the wound to guarantee a free flow of blood. The blood itself is lapped up with the tongue. Vampires have better vision than most other bats, but travel about in search of hosts only during the darkest hours – they appear to avoid moonlit nights except in Hollywood. In floodplain forests they live in the hollows of trees, usually not too far from the water's edge, as rivers and lakes are the nocturnal highways they use to move about within their home ranges.

Bats are the second most diverse mammalian group in the world, surpassed only by the rodents. Whereas most of the rodent diversity is dependent, nutritionally, on plant matter of some sort, overall bat diversity is closely linked to insect life. Most bats in the world are insectivorous. In rainforests, however, where bat diversity per given area is higher than anywhere else, over half of the species are fruit-, nectar- or pollen-feeders. Rainforest bats and plants have evolved mutual relationships. The plants provide the food for bats, and the animals in turn either pollinate the flowers or disperse the seeds to new sites.

In the Old World the plant-eating bats are the so-called flying foxes. This group of bats, however, did not disperse into the New World. With the fruit, nectar and pollen resources available, New World plant-eating bats evolved from a largely insectivorous group, the spear-nosed bats, named after the shape of the snout found in most species. It is also the largest family of the region. The fruit-eating bats of the Old World, the flying foxes, use vision rather than echo-location to navigate. The spear-nosed bats, like most of their insectivorous relatives, rely mostly on echo-location to navigate.

Around Manaus, in the heart of the Amazon, there are more than 50 bat species, of which 60 per cent are spear-nosed bats feeding principally on fleshy fruits, and probably also on nectar and pollen, though this has been little investigated. In the floodplains, for example, fruit is only available in large quantities during the flooding season, thus at other times of the year bats must either migrate elsewhere, change diets or in some cases hibernate. It is likely that migration and diet shifts are the main adaptations practised by bats found on floodplains. The Amazonian bat fauna has been too little investigated to know if there are species restricted just to floodplains. More likely, all, or nearly all, of the floodplain species can also be found in upland forest as well.

The spear-nosed bats are important flower pollinators and seed dispersal agents in Amazonian flooded forests. Flower nectar is mainly a carbohydrate, whereas pollen is a good source of protein. The nectar-feeding bats have undergone various anatomical modifications in order to reach the nectaries of flowers. Their most outstanding characteristics are their relatively long snouts and long tongues. Their tongues are endowed with greatly lengthened papillae (protuberances) that form a kind of mop for sopping up nectar. Bat-pollinated rainforest plants include trees, lianas and epiphytes whose flowers hang on stout peduncles (stalks) so that the flying animals can clear the surrounding branches and leaves. Alternatively, the flowers may be clustered at the end of branches so that a bat can use this inflorescence as a landing pad, and subsequently move about it feeding on nectar and pollen. This is the case with the bat-pollinated flowers of the kapok (silk-cotton) tree.

Many trees in Amazonian flooded forests lose their leaves, at least for a brief period, when they are flowering and this may indicate they are bat-pollinated plants. The leafless condition appears to allow freer bat navigation. Bats are known to fly many kilometres during a night from one food source to the next, thus they make good pollinators since they carry pollen that has become attached to their bodies.

Seed dispersal by bats is carried out when the animals eat at one site and then defecate at another. There is plenty of evidence that gut passage does not destroy most seeds and, by scoring the seeds, it may even promote germination. Because Amazonian flooded forests have a large number of potential seed dispersal agents, bats share this ecological role with birds and mammals in the canopy and fish in the water. In the upland area near Manaus, the seeds of over 35 plant species are known to be dispersed by bats. Figs and the fruits of umbrella trees (*Cecropia*) are the two most common groups of Amazonian flooded plants whose seeds are regularly dispersed by bats.

The insect-feeding bats also find a home in flooded forests but, as with many Amazonian animals, little is yet known about their behaviour. Those that feed on insects and that are seen in the *igapó* include the sheathed-tailed, disk-winged, vesper and free-tailed bats. Like predaceous spiders and ants, perhaps they find more insects when the floods come and their prey becomes concentrated in the middle and upper canopy region.

The flying animals are not the only large species of the flooded forest canopy. There is in addition a wide diversity of non-flying vertebrates that have conquered the flooded forest on four limbs.

CHAPTER FOUR

FEET
IN THE
FOREST

In rainforest canopies most of the vertebrate animals that cannot fly move around on four feet. Snakes, of course, are the exception. Worm-lizards are also legless, but they do not climb trees. The four-footed animals include the mammals – other than bats – amphibians and reptiles. Primates and frogs are the most diverse groups of flooded forest quadrupeds, each with at least 20 known species from the *igapó*. Lizards are relatively well represented but little is yet known about most of the smaller species in the canopy. In addition to their four feet, many canopy quadrupeds have a fifth limb, that is, a prehensile tail. No fauna in any other region in the world has as many prehensile-tailed animals as that of the Amazonian rainforest. The prehensile tail has evolved independently in at least four major mammalian groups, including the New World primates, some rodents, a few racoon-like animals and opossums.

The New World monkeys have evolved into two main groups, and the Amazon Basin is the major centre of this primate diversity. There are around 40 monkey species in the Amazon Basin and at least 70 distinct forms of these. The small marmosets and tamarins, whose average adult size is only around 300 grammes, are all arboreal and active diurnally (by day). Most of the species live in small groups consisting of a monogamous breeding pair and their offspring. Anatomically they are distinct from all other monkeys in the world because their digits, with the exception of the first toe which ends in a flat nail, terminate in curved claws. These claws, as we will see shortly, allow them to practice a habit reminiscent of Amazonian rubber collectors.

The cebids, including the capuchins, howlers and many other subgroups, are generally much larger monkeys than the marmosets and tamarins and, of all the South American primates, they have the largest brains and most closely resem-

ble the African apes. The cebids are represented by no fewer than 20 species in the Amazon Basin.

Very few Amazonian primates descend to the ground on a regular basis, or have any need to. Lack of water during the dry season in some Amazonian areas appears to be the chief reason why monkeys, other than the uakaris, occasionally leave the trees. Most of the time, sufficient water can be tapped from succulent vegetation sources in the canopy or from rain dripping from the trees. The fact that huge areas of forest are seasonally inundated along Amazonian rivers has little direct effect on the arboreal primates, since they live in the canopy and thus, for the most part, above flood levels. Furthermore, because the floodplain and upland forest canopies are interconnected, monkeys and other animals have a continuous arboreal highway between the two major vegetation types. Most of the species make use of it, at least on a seasonal basis in their search for food.

Though floodplain forests account for only about 2 per cent of the total Amazonian rainforest, because of the vastness of the system their ecological role in monkey natural history is much greater than this proportion may suggest. Floodplain forests have a relatively intense fruiting period, lasting between the beginning and the peak of the annual floods. It appears that floodplain fruit crops, at least for many plant groups, are greater than in upland forests. The combination of intense fruiting and thus greater abundance per given area works like an advertisement to attract large numbers of monkeys and other fruit-eating animals from the adjacent upland areas to the inundation zones. Geographically, this ecological displacement of fruit-eating arboreal animals, within the rainforest in general, is enhanced by the complex, almost cobweb-like river system. The thousands of peninsulas formed where any two rivers meet greatly decreases the distances that migratory arboreal animals have to travel to be within accessible reach of floodplain forests when they are inundated, and when they are mostly in fruit. In the Amazonian Lowlands, perhaps the furthest an animal could ever get from a flooded forest would be about 200 kilometres, and usually no more than 50–100 kilometres, all within seasonal migratory distances.

Few if any major Amazonian monkey groups are totally absent from flooded forests, or at least the edges of rivers, though local distribution patterns vary greatly. However, the main reasons for this are so far not understood and relatively few areas have been investigated.

The smallest monkey in the world, the pygmy marmoset, is found only in the upper Amazon Basin where it lives mostly in floodplain areas or along the edges of rivers. It appears to be the most successful of its family in flooded forests. The other two Amazonian marmosets, the tassel-ear and bare-ear, are only found east of the Madeira and south of the Amazon River and, for the most part, out of the Amazonian Lowlands, thus far away from flooded forests. The tamarins are the most diverse group of small monkeys in the Amazon and, though some of the species are found in flooded forests or along the edges of rivers, little is known about them.

The extremely small size of the pygmy marmoset, which would make it an attractive target for birds of prey, necessitates a life restricted mostly to the middle and lower canopies where it is more hidden and difficult to catch. At night it takes to holes where it tucks itself away out of reach of most predators. Social groups of up to 15 individuals are observed, and these consist of a monogamous breeding pair and their offspring. Twins are the rule, and the father participates extensively in the care of the young.

Pygmy marmosets are omnivorous feeders, but they have developed one habit, the tapping of saps and gums, to an extent unknown elsewhere in primates. Their almost chisel-like incisor teeth allow them to gouge holes in bark, sometimes in areas already injured by insects, to start a flow of tree fluids on which they feed. Their claw-like nails, along with small body size, provide the additional adaptations needed to forage saps and gums on vertical trunks, feeding habitats on which there are few if any major competitors. Pygmy marmoset families have very small home ranges, usually less than a third of a hectare, but on which there may be several large trees marked by their oval-shaped gouges.

Latex-tapping by Amazonian rubber collectors reminds one of pygmy marmoset behaviour. Whereas marmosets gnaw oval gouges into the bark to start gums or saps flowing, rubber collectors slice the trees diagonally, placing a small cup at the bottom of the cut to capture the white latex that drips out. Both rubber collectors and marmosets must be careful not to over-tap the trees, lest they kill them and hence destroy the resource on which they depend. Thus the gouges and cuts found on Amazonian floodplain trees are the economic initials of a lower and higher primate whose behaviours have converged, though for different reasons.

Of the larger non-human primates, the squirrel monkey is the mostly commonly seen species in flooded forests, though it is by no means restricted to this habitat. The squirrel monkey is at home in many different kinds of habitat, from low to high and dry to wet tropical forest. Its broad adaptability is the principal reason why, of all the Amazon monkeys found in floodplain forests, it is the one that perhaps adapts best to areas that have been highly disturbed by Man.

The squirrel monkey is very inquisitive of human activities and will often peer down, apparently not frightened by the similar but larger type of animal it sees paddling through the flooded forest in a canoe. Though they are good jumpers, they seem to prefer running along branches rather than long leaps from one tree to the next.

Squirrel monkeys represent the largest groups of non-human primates, with perhaps an average of 20–50 individuals per troop. Troops of up to a 100 individuals are known. In flooded forests they appear to stick mostly to the average. Birth in flooded forest populations appears to take place at about the beginning of the floods, remembering that this also coincides with the fruiting season. Adult females form the core of the groups and prefer each other's company to that of the males. When a female has no young, she will often help a mother with newborn, and this generally involves carrying the infants about on her back.

Squirrel monkeys are very omnivorous, though they show a strong preference for fruit when it is available. The group will often spread out in the middle and upper canopy layers in search of food, drawing together once a source has been located. They are one of the most dexterous monkeys and are known to take insects on the wing. Insects, spiders and other invertebrates, along with small vertebrates and their eggs, are all welcome food. They often watch birds nesting, such as the large hoatzin, and when the nests are unattended they will snatch up the eggs. In fact they are probably among the main bird-egg predators in some flooded forests.

All of the monkeys of the world, with one exception, are diurnal. This exception is the night monkey, a species widely distributed in South and part of Central America. Its extremely large eyes are, superficially, more reminiscent of those of an owl than of other monkeys. The night monkey is relatively common in the flooded forests of some Amazonian rivers, whereas it seems to be completely missing in others. Its presence, however, is easily detected when the moon is full or nearly so for it is only under a bright night sky that it calls. To the human listener its hoots appear somewhat mournful. Only the male hoots in an attempt to attract mates or to establish territories. Night monkeys live on a diet of fruits, leaves, nectar and insects, and they appear to use all the layers of the forest during their foraging. Bats are their main fruit-eating peers at night in flooded forests.

Species pairs – one found in flooded areas, the other on high ground – are common in both the animal and plant kingdoms in the Amazon Basin. In the highly mobile arboreal fauna, of which monkeys are outstanding examples, it is not always clear whether the ecological separation is maintained because of physiological reasons or because of competitive exclusion. Physical barriers could not be a factor as monkeys can pass easily from upland to flooded forests. Competitive exclusion suggests that one species prevents, through some kind of competition, subtle or direct, another closely related form from invading its habitat. Thus excluded, theoretically scarce resources do not need to be shared. Titi monkeys present this pattern in the Amazon.

The dusky titi is most closely associated with swampy areas where the vegetation is waterlogged for much of the year. Heavy flooding, along with poor, often sandy soils, results in vegetation low in stature and often quite thick as a result of numerous thin trees and many vines. It is in this habitat that the dusky titi is most at home. The widow titi, on the other hand, lives mostly in the stunted forests growing in the white sand areas that are interspersed through much of the Amazonian rainforest. When the dusky titi is absent from swampy areas, however, the widow titi will move into these habitats.

Titi monkeys are difficult to observe as they stay hidden in the dense vegetation where they live. Groups consist only of families comprising the two adults and their offspring. Unique among monkeys is their habit of tail-twining when at rest. This behaviour may increase balance when the monkeys sleep on a branch, and it probably also strengthens pair bonding. Male titis are perhaps the most attentive of all primate fathers. From the second day on, except when feeding, babies are carried by the father. Dusky titis feed mostly on fruits, but also obtain much if not most of their protein from leaves, leaf stalks and young shoots. The widow titis, however, living in the sandy soil vegetation areas, where leaves are often hard and perhaps more toxic, largely substitute insects and other invertebrates for leaves. In contrast to the dusky titis in their dense vegetation, widow titis prefer the open areas above the upper canopy where they can keep an eye out for danger.

The millions of tons of leaves in a rainforest represent a potentially huge food resource for primates and other animals. Many Old World monkeys rely heavily on leaves for the bulk of their diets, but few New World primate groups have the physiological adaptations required to digest fibrous cellulose. Furthermore, rainforest leaves in general are low in nutrients per volume of digestible fibre and very low in sugars. Fruits, of course, have a high sugar content, and this largely explains why most New World monkeys eat them instead of leaves.

Howler monkeys are also highly dependent on fruits but, more than other New World primates, they can, when their favourite food is not available, turn to large quantities of leaves, which they are able to digest with the help of cellulolytic bacteria found in their hindgut. Leaf-eating perhaps explains why howlers, where they occur, represent the highest percentage of the primate population in Amazonian rainforests. Whereas other monkeys might be limited by the availability of fruits and invertebrates, howlers substitute leaves.

Howlers are by far the loudest of New World primates. Their reverberating howls are produced by forcing air through a cavity in the enlarged hyoid bone at the base of the tongue. This apparatus is much larger in males whose uproar is used to defend territories, since vocalization is cheaper, energetically, than physical combat. Howling begins at dawn as a signal of whereabouts to other nearby troops. When moving on during the day the troop will howl again in order to avoid conflict with other groups and to establish feeding territories, though these often overlap to some extent.

Of the three species of howlers in the Amazon, only the red howler is commonly seen in flooded forests. It lives mostly in areas of tall virgin forest. It does not adapt well to disturbed areas, and that is why it is not often seen along much of the Amazon River. Also, it has been much hunted for food.

The steady but usually slow progression of the howler through forests, often taking many days to cover its home range, is tied to its search for edible leaves, on which about half its diet depends. It makes much use of its prehensile tail, the last underneath quarter of which consists of a pad of bare skin. When feeding or sleeping, howlers anchor themselves to branches by their dexterous tails.

Socially, howlers are one of the least developed monkey species found in Amazonian flooded forests. They have relatively small brains for their body size and social interactions are low-key compared to most other Amazonian monkeys. They nevertheless live in relatively permanent, tight groups of up to 20 individuals. When a male takes over a new group, he may begin his reign by killing the infants.

Few animals have the physical and physiological adaptations to turn most of what they see into potential food. Of Amazonian monkeys, the capuchins have evolved furthest in that direction. Flooded forest troops, often reaching a dozen individuals, will spread out from near the water to the upper canopy in search of food. Two species are found in the Amazonian Lowlands, and these only occur together south of the Amazon River. The brown capuchin ranges throughout the Amazon Basin, whereas the white-fronted capuchin has not made it north of the Amazon River.

Capuchins are extremely intelligent animals, and that impression is enhanced by the curious manner in which they appear to observe and scrutinize, and sometimes even jeer, as one travels by canoe through the flooded forest. Feeding sessions look like raids, as the monkeys search for almost anything that is edible. Fruit is usually the main item in their diets, though they are also fond of flowers and young leaf shoots. While feeding on flowers, these monkeys are also pollinators, as they move from bloom to bloom in search of nectar and young buds. Capuchins, with their dexterous hands, are able to break open tough tusked fruits. They often beat fruits together or smash them against trunks to get at the seeds, or fleshy material surrounding the seeds. On the animal side, they regularly attack insects and spiders, often opening up rotting wood, digging under bark and poking into the bases of palm fronds and bromeliads to dislodge their food. Bird eggs and chicks fit the menu, as do small lizards and even arboreal rodents. They are also reported to take small monkeys.

Saki monkeys in general appear to avoid swampy areas. The black-bearded saki, when found in flooded forests, usually sticks relatively close to nearby upland forest. The white-nosed saki which is found between the Xingu and Madeira Rivers uses both upland and floodplain forests, where it remains mostly in the upper canopy levels, only very seldom descending to lower levels. Most of its diet is comprised of fruits but, unlike other fruit-eating monkeys, with the exception of the uakari, it eats large quantities of immature seeds. During the rainy season, when fleshy fruits are abundant, it subsists mostly on pulp material. Little fleshy fruit is available during the dry season, and at that time the white-nosed saki turns to immature seeds. White-nosed sakis have been observed queueing at palm trees armed with dangerous spines. Each individual takes its turn descending to the palm crown, picking its fruit and then removing itself to an adjacent tree to feed.

Though Amazonian rainforests, including those on the floodplains, have a great diversity of fruit-eating animals, few species are able to deal with large fruits with tough husks, of which there are a great variety. The largest fruit-eating primates of the Amazon are the woolly, spider and uakari monkeys. The woolly monkey is rarely seen on floodplains, unless kept there as a pet. The black spider monkey, ranging from upland to floodplain habitats of tall forest, attacks large fruits but does not seem to be able to cope with the tough-husked species. The uakari monkeys, along with the macaws and some of the larger parrots, are the most highly specialized animals in flooded forests for opening up tough-husked fruits to get at the seeds or fleshy material within.

Perhaps the only Amazonian monkeys that confine themselves to forests subject to seasonal flooding are the uakaris. The behaviour of these monkeys has been a mystery until just recently, though naturalists had reported on them in the last century. Thanks to a long-term study of the bald uakari by Dr Márcio Ayres, the most mysterious monkey has become the Amazon's best known primate.

The bald uakari is strikingly different from all other primates in its hairless and red face. Its face is about the colour of the European tourists one sees roasting themselves under the tropical sun on the roof deck of boats travelling the Amazon. Smarter than tourists, the bald uakari prefers the shade of the forest. The red face pokes out of a shaggy body coat that varies between white and red depending on the geographical location. The function of uakari baldness is still unclear.

The white-haired bald uakari has one of the most restricted distributions of any known Amazonian primate. It is found in the delta-like area formed where the Rio Japurá, a leftbank tributary, meets the Amazon River, and southwestward to a yet unknown extent. It appears to stick to geologically young floodplain that is mostly covered by high forest. It is still unknown, and perhaps never will be known, whether this area represents a refuge for this species, forced or restricted there by the other uakari forms. Again, it may be that the white-haired race evolved only recently there and has not yet spread elsewhere.

The white-haired bald uakari spends its day roughly in thirds – travelling, feeding and sleeping. Feeding troops average around eight individuals. Uakaris are the great leapers of the flooded forest. They have been observed to leap 20–30 metres as they travel from tree to tree in search of edible fruits and seeds. Unlike many of the other Amazonian monkeys that are great leapers, they do not have a prehensile tail, but rather a short one that they use to brace themselves. Uakaris often use three of their limbs in a tripod fashion to brace themselves. The one free hand is used for feeding. They are highly adapted for splitting open large fruits, from which they remove the seeds or fleshy material with their incisor teeth. Uakaris subsist, probably more than any other New World monkey group, on a diet of fruits and seeds. Perhaps 85 per cent of their diet consists of fruit.

Mature floodplain fruit, however, is mostly available only during the rainy season, or the time of the floods. To find sufficient quantities of fruit, the uakaris must also eat immature fruits and seeds, many of which are probably toxic to other animals. During low water, when fruits are scarce, the uakaris will leave the trees and move to the ground in search of fallen seeds or to uproot recently germinated seedlings. Some individuals, however, stay in the trees as guards. In smaller floodplain areas, peccaries, tapirs and rodents soon colonize the forest, as river level falls, to feed on the fruits and seeds left behind by the water. Ground foraging by white-haired bald uakaris may be due to the general absence of these large mammals in the floodplain areas where the monkeys are found.

Animals that live an arboreal and terrestrial existence would be expected to have relatively broad feeding habits. The ringtailed coati, found throughout much of South America, is such an animal in the Amazonian flooded forest. Unlike any of the other members of the racoon family, the coati is diurnal. When out of sight, bands of them moving through flooded forest can easily be mistaken for monkeys. The bands consist solely of females and their young, as adult males are solitary.

Like many of the South American monkeys, coatis have long tails which they can effectively use as a fifth limb for balancing when climbing. They also have long claws as do some monkeys but, unlike other arboreal animals in the flooded forest, they have reversible ankles which allow them to descend trees head first. When the floodplain forests are not inundated, the coatis move down to the ground to feed on insects, small invertebrates and fallen fruit. They find most of their animal food by snuffling in litter and rotten wood with their long snouts. When confined to the trees during the floods, they appear to rely more on fruit than insects as food.

One of the least known animals in the Amazonian forest is the rarely seen kinkajou, related to the coati and other racoon-like animals. The kinkajou is known for its long tongue, which it uses to feed on flower nectar and perhaps honey, and for its prehensile tail. The kinkajou is thought to be mostly a fruit-eater.

Squirrels are among the most successful seed-eating animals in many of the world's forests. In the world's greatest forest, the Amazonian rainforest, they face much competition from other seed-eating animals, and only a member of the red squirrel group is commonly seen in floodplain areas.

The rodent most commonly seen and heard in the flooded forest is the toró spiny rat. Its loud calls – tow-row! . . . tow-row! . . . tow-row! – are among the strangest of the *igapó*, and give it its common name. It can be heard calling day or night, but it is most active nocturnally. During the day it lives in trunk holes, though it is also often seen resting on high branches. The toró appears to feed mostly on vegetable matter, and adapts to disturbed floodplain areas as long as some forest is left.

If an animal is relatively heavy and slow, it pays to have some kind of defensive armour. In floodplain waters, turtles illustrate this point. In the trees above, prehensile-tailed porcupines are an even more pointed case. Though prehensile-tailed porcupines look clumsy, they are nevertheless excellent climbers. Their grip in trees is enhanced by the callus-padded end of the tail which they curl around branches. They are nocturnal and omnivorous in habit, relying, however, mostly on leaves and fruits. They do not see well, but make up for it through keen senses of touch, smell and hearing. They are able to pass the flooding season in the trees, and it is still unclear to what extent they descend to the forest floor to feed when the floodplains are drained.

Prehensile-tailed porcupines are occasionally seen swimming in floodplain areas or even crossing small rivers. In some areas red-bellied piranhas attack them when they cross lakes. The piranhas, however, end up with spines perforating their stomachs, though, miraculously, many of these predators appear to survive their wounds. Another predator that attacks the porcupines is the harpy eagle and the giant bird can swallow the spines apparently with little, if any, injury to itself.

The tamanduá anteater is a good example of an animal that can live in many different kinds of habitats, though in each it is highly specialized to feed on ants and termites, which it laps up with its long tongue. Of course ants and termites are common insects almost everywhere in the American tropics, thus anteaters have been guaranteed food in habitats ranging from savannas to rainforest. When Amazonian floodplain forests are first inundated, ants often become very concentrated on tree trunks and branches as they move upwards to escape drowning. This concentration of ants often attracts tamanduá anteaters to the floodplains, at least for a couple of months each year. In some floodplain areas, termite nests in the trees are also common, and these animals also become more concentrated during floods when they too must abandon submerged trails.

The tamanduá and silky anteaters, in contrast to the giant anteaters, are largely nocturnal animals. They are usually found alone and prefer the trees to the ground. Flooding presents no problem to them since they can move from tree to tree when foraging. On the ground they are clumsy, but in the trees, with the aid of their prehensile tails, they can move quite rapidly. Tamanduá anteaters will also feed on nectar and fruit material, but the extent to which this is done is still not known.

The silky anteater is about the size of a small house cat and, unlike the tamanduá and giant anteaters, it appears to avoid feeding on termites. It does feed heavily on ants, however, but also probably takes more fruit and other vegetable material than its relatives.

Most of the larger mammals that live in the Amazonian rainforest canopy can move fast, at least over short distances, to escape predators if need be. Like almost every general trend in natural history, however, there are major exceptions. Sloths are the slowest of the slow, but in many floodplain areas they probably account, in total weight, for the largest single percentage of mammalian weight.

The success of sloths in the tropical American rainforest is undoubtedly due in large part to their position in the foodweb and their ability to hide from predators. Blue-green algae grow in the hair grooves of sloths, thus camouflaging the coat against the green foliage in which the animal lives. They have perhaps the most highly developed adaptations for leaf-eating of any mammal found in Amazonian floodplain forests. Their stomachs are divided into many digestive compartments that contain cellulose-digesting bacteria. A low metabolic rate, combined with minimum movement, conserves energy. Leaf-eaters in general must consume large quantities of their food to satisfy their nutritional requirements. A third of the weight of a sloth can be made up of leaves. Furthermore, leaves may last up to a month in the intestines. Faeces and urine are passed about once a week at habitual places in each sloth's territory. Perhaps this helps to recycle nutrients more efficiently to their food trees or enables them to keep away from excrement and urine that might attract predators or parasites. Flooded forest sloths, however, cannot descend to the ground during the floods and it appears that they defecate just above the water. The young are carried by the female for up to nine months and after weaning they also feed while clinging to the mother.

Sloths are excellent if slow swimmers. They are known, for reasons still only privy to them, to cross rivers, even the Amazon River. In some cases, it must take them several hours to make a crossing. The fact that rivers are not barriers to them helps explain why they are so widely distributed. In flooded forest they will unhesitatingly swim from one food tree to the next, usually only a short distance, if they cannot reach their destination via the canopy.

The night monkey is the only nocturnal monkey in the world. At night it forages for a wide range of plant and animal foods and faces little competition from other monkeys.

Overleaf left: Titis are small monkeys, and often hide in thick vegetation in flooded forests where they avoid potential predators more easily. They feed mostly on fruit and young leaves.
Overleaf right: One of the great mysteries of the flooded forest is how the trees survive the absence of oxygen in the root zone.

Floodplain forests are the home to both the three-toed and two-toed sloths. As does its relative, the two-toed sloth has three digits on the forelimbs but, unlike it, only two on the hindlimbs. The three-toed sloth is the species most commonly seen in Amazonian floodplain habitats because it is active diurnally as well as nocturnally. The larger two-toed sloth is nocturnal and appears to have a much more patchy distribution. The three-toed sloth also adapts better to floodplain areas highly disturbed by Man.

Opossums are survivors from the clash of marsupial and placental mammals in the South American theatre. As discussed in Chapter 1, for much of its geological history, South America was isolated from Central and North America by a waterway in what is now the Isthmus of Panama region. With the lowering of sea levels about 2–5 million years ago, South America became connected to the northern landmass. There was a subsequent dispersal – some call it invasion – of northern placental mammals into South America. For reasons that are still not clear most of the South American marsupials were replaced by placental mammals. The only marsupials to survive were the opossums and shrew opossums, the latter restricted to the Andes. Opossums, however, also broke out of South America and subsequently dispersed as far north as Virginia and Ohio.

Opossums are, above all, opportunists. Most of the species, and there are at least five or six in flooded forests, are adapted to feed on a wide variety of foods, including fruits, seeds, small vertebrates and many kinds of invertebrates. The four-eyed, mouse, black-shouldered, woolly, and bushy-tailed opossums are good climbers and highly adapted to an arboreal life. Many species are found together in flooded forests, but individuals for the most part lead a solitary life and direct conflict between species appears to be rare. The various species, when living in the same area, inhabit different layers of the forest. Some of the species readily become scavengers on human garbage, and also take to killing small chickens at night, thus making them unpopular with floodplain peasants.

Living in the trees of Amazonian flooded forests are large *jacuruxi*-lizards (family Teiidae) which could at first glance be mistaken for small caimans of about a metre's length. These semi-aquatic lizards do in fact have several features that are reminiscent of crocodilians, such as the ridged scales of their bodies which in the tail region form a dorsal and lateral keel that merges as the tail becomes narrow. *Jacuruxi*-lizards have strong jaws but much blunter teeth than caimans. Unlike the iguanas, *jacuruxi*-lizards forage underwater as well as in the trees and are thus nicely adapted to a life in the *igapó*. In the whitewater river areas where calcium and other minerals are sufficient to support relatively large mollusk populations, the large lizards appear to feed heavily on snails. The lizards walk along the bottom or swim through the flooded forest in search of snails and other large invertebrates. The prey is brought to the surface, crushed and the soft parts removed. In the *igapó* forest trees, especially during the dry

The three monkeys that are most restricted to flooded forests are the red uakari (top), white uakari (opposite) and pygmy marmoset (above). The pygmy marmoset is also the smallest monkey in the world.

Overleaf: Shrub communities often grow along the river channel edge of flooded forest. Shrubs can be flooded for up to 8–11 months each year and must flower and fruit in the short period when they are emerged during the low water period.

The canopy of the flooded forest is used in many different ways by animals. The three-toed sloth
(top) and red howler monkey (opposite) both feed on leaves. The first has a relatively restricted
territory whereas the latter ranges widely in search of its food. The arowhana fish (above) jumps
out of the water to take beetles and other prey perched on overhanging vegetation in the flooded forest.

Overleaf: Many flooded forests in the Amazon are open enough for a naturalist in a dugout
canoe, accompanied by a native paddleman, to travel relatively freely through this world of water and trees.

Long tails are an important adaptation for many animals in the rainforest. Squirrel monkeys (top) and the ring-tailed coati (opposite) have prehensile tails which they use as a fifth limb for support in the trees. The large teiid lizard (above) falls out of the tops of the trees and into the water when danger approaches. It uses its long tail for slowing the fall and for balance.

Other than the rainforest trees themselves, various types of plants that grow on them are important habitats for animals. Bromeliads (above) are especially important in some flooded forests as they provide cover and water. Because of predatory fish, most flooded forest frogs, such as the barred leaf frog (top) and Phyllomedusa frogs (opposite), live on the trees rather than in the water.

phase, the large lizards forage for arboreal invertebrates, eggs and other animal prey rather than venture too far into river channels or floodplain lakes where they might be taken by other large predators, such as caimans, anacondas and some fish species. It is still not known whether they eat vegetable matter and, as their diets probably overlap very little with the more or less vegetarian iguanas, the two groups of large lizards live comfortably with each other in these forests.

Iguanas (family Iguandidae) are more common in flooded forests than *jacuruxi*-lizards and easily distinguished from them by their generally green rather than brown colours. Brazilian Amazonians call the large iguana the *chamaleāo*, a name the Portuguese borrowed from another family of lizards, the chameleons, living in the Old World. Like the Old World chameleons, iguanas can change colour – usually some combination of green, dark green or brown – to blend better into their environment. They have extremely long toes and nails that allow them to climb easily in trees and their tails are usually longer than their bodies. The largest species reaches nearly 2 metres in length. The species found in the flooded forests also occur in upland forest.

Iguanas commonly climb to the tops of the *igapó* trees where they bask on exposed branches, though they use the entire canopy in their food searches. When danger approaches they show two responses. From the bottom part of the head hangs a huge appendage, the gular sack, which the animal inflates when irritated or frightened or during sexual displays. At the same time, it raises its dorsal crest which looks like a comb with teeth becoming gradually smaller from the head to the tail. Iguanas also have the curious ability to fall out of the tops of trees, sometimes 20–30 metres, and land on the ground or in the water without injury. The strong, large and well protected tail catches branches during the descent, thus greatly breaking the speed of the fall. Iguanas swim very well so falling into the water is no problem to them. It is not an uncommon experience in the *igapó* forest to approach a tree where iguanas are feeding and all of the sudden see them fall out of the canopy and splash into the water, sometimes quite close to the canoe.

As mentioned, iguanas are much more vegetarian than the *jacuruxi*-lizards and feed on leaf-shoots, fruit pulp and flowers, though they also take invertebrates, bird eggs and other animal prey. Unlike many other places in Latin America, iguanas are not commonly included in the human diet of the Amazon.

Amazonian floodplain frogs are much more abundant in open habitats, such as the floating meadows we will explore later, than in flooded forest. At the time the floods arrive, and also when they retreat, there are many pools scattered about the *igapó* that would seem ideal for frog reproduction. Nevertheless, frog breeding choruses are rarely heard in these forest pools. The pools, however, usually contain at least several voracious fish species, especially the highly predaceous *traíra* characins (*Hoplias*). *Traíra* found in forest pools range from the young to adults in excess of 30–40 centimetres in length and they are highly adapted to live in only a few centimetres of water, usually under the forest leaf litter. They attack almost any animal that they can swallow, and it is this behaviour that has placed the flooded forest pools off-limits to frogs that might otherwise breed in these habitats. Moreover, there is no evidence that any frog species breeds in the *igapó* waters during the main floods.

Almost nothing is yet known about the frogs that live in the flooded forest canopy, or how and where they breed. Some probably breed in bromeliads when rainwater fills their leaf bowls. In the Amazonian rainforest in general, diurnal frogs are leaf-litter species that spend the night on understorey plants, usually herbaceous forms no more than a metre above the floor. The inundation of the flooded forest appears to preclude most of these species, though they are often abundant enough at the non-flooded edge of the *igapó*. Flooded forest frogs are largely nocturnal and arboreal and still await a naturalist to study them.

Igapó forest represents the 'green mansions' of Amazonian floodplains. But, as we saw earlier, trees have only been successful where flooding is not too deep and where the floodplains are drained for at least a short period each year. On the floodplains of some Amazonian rivers grows another type of vegetation in addition to the flooded forests. Let us now explore this other habitat which provides additional opportunities for floodplain life.

CHAPTER FIVE

RAFTS

OF

LIFE

Along Amazonian shores and floodplains, especially those of the muddy rivers carrying nutrient-enriched silt out of the Andes, are sprawling communities of herbaceous plants. These are the river meadows, verdant carpets of grasses, sedges and broad-leaved floating plants whose seasonal expansions and contractions are tuned to the rhythms of water level fluctuation. The two major life forms are free-floating plants whose roots dangle in the water and those that are rooted in the bottom sediments. Very few of the river meadow species remain completely submerged, as light conditions in general in Amazonian rivers are too poor to allow much photosynthesis below the surface. Furthermore, the emerged species colonize most of the space available for herbaceous plants and prevent the submerged forms from developing to any great extent.

By floating or growing upwards with rising water levels, the river meadows are guaranteed their places in the sun. Floating plants, of course, can deal very easily with rising river levels as they ride passively on top of the floods. Herbaceous plants rooted in the sediments, however, must be able to grow as fast as river level rises. This can be as much as 20 centimetres a day, or about 3 metres a month at the beginning of the floods. In odd years when river level rises much faster than the average, the rooted plants lose the race upwards. If their stems and leaves do not remain at least a little above the surface they cannot photosynthesize fast enough to provide the upward growth that guarantees their survival. When this happens they are much reduced in quantity, though when normal floods return they re-enter the race in the form of seedlings that recolonize the same areas during the dry season.

Very few of the floodplain species with roots in the soil opt not to grow upwards with the floods. Those that do not, of course, must spend the high water period dormant. They flourish during the emerged months, though only in areas that remain somewhat boggy. In some cases the emerged floodplains during the dry phase are colonized by terrestrial herbaceous plants recruited through wind and animal dispersal from adjacent upland communities. This type of colonization has become especially common where agriculture and cattle ranching has led to much dry season burning, thus eliminating the natural vegetation and allowing the invasion of what are really weeds. The floods, however, wipe out the weeds.

When the water level drops and much if not most of the river banks and floodplains are left drained, the herbaceous plants dry out and drop to the ground where most of the stem and leaf matter begins to decompose or, perhaps even more likely, it is swept away to the river channels and carried downstream. Many species, and especially the grasses, set seed just before the end of the floods, and the water disperses these seeds far and wide. Most of the rooted species also sprout from remnant adult plants that survive the dry season on the floodplain floor.

One of the richest habitats in all the Amazon is formed by floating islands of herbaceous plants and the organic material they accumulate. The floating meadows can reach over a kilometre in length and several hundred metres in width. The tops of the floating meadows are colonized by non-floating, largely terrestrial species, such as passion fruit and morning glory vines (among many other creepers and climbers) as well as sedges, arums and some small terrestrial shrubs and small trees.

The most majestic floating plant in the Amazon is the giant water lily. Ironically, the Latin scientific name, *Victoria regia*, that for more than a century was used to identify this beautiful plant and from which one of its common names, the Queen Victoria water lily, was derived, has recently been shown to be incorrect. The correct Latin name is *Victoria amazonica*. Amazonians, however, call the lily *vitoria regia*, and thus it shall remain in vernacular if not scientific nomenclature.

The giant lily is found mostly in fully lit, quiet backwaters of the muddy river floodplain lakes. These lakes, however, often become somewhat transparent when the sediments have sunk to the bottom. The giant lily's huge saucer-shaped leaves can reach nearly 2 metres in diameter whereas the large white flowers, buoyed on their own stems, can attain the size of an adult human head. With low water the lily pads and stems are usually left on dry ground where they decompose. The root base, however, often remains alive and new stems sprout from it with the next floods. The stems and leaves can grow several centimetres per day to accompany rising water levels up to a maximum depth of about 5 metres. The lilies are seldom found in waters deeper than this.

The floating flowers of the giant lily are present throughout much of the flooding season and they open at dusk. This activity is very impressive when there are hundreds flowers opening at about the same time in a large lily patch. As the flowers open, their internal temperature rises by as much as 11°C and they also begin to emit a strong odour, like butterscotch or pineapple. Various scarab beetles are attracted by a combination of the white flowers and their strong scent. The beetles enter the flowers where they spend the night. By sunrise the flowers close and the beetles are trapped within. While imprisoned, however, the beetles feed on the spongy, swollen starchy tissue of the carpels, that is, the seed-bearing organs of the flower. Once the carpel appendages have been eaten, the stamens hang loosely inwards and their pollen-bearing anthers split open. This causes the pollen to be scattered all over the stamens. Moving about inside the flower the beetles become completely covered with pollen. About 16-18 hours after the flowers have opened their petals change colour from a white to a dark purplish-red and the petals and sepals open enough to release the beetles.

The released and pollen-carrying beetles then search for a new first-night lily flower which they enter, but this time they also cross-pollinate it. The beetles are not attracted to second-night flowers because these are no longer scented, they have changed to a colour that is no longer inviting and they are not heated. As flowering takes place over a long period during the flooding season, nearly all of the flowers get pollinated by the beetles.

Subsequent to its second night of opening, and the release of the imprisoned and pollinating beetles, the large flowers slowly sink to the bottom of the lake. As the flowers decompose underwater the seeds mature within a pod. The pod eventually decomposes as well and the seeds are released and float to the surface where they are dispersed by water until they sink a few days later.

The giant lily pads are used by many animal species. One of the most peculiar, and certainly the noisiest, is the jacana. Jacanas are unique birds because of their extremely long toes and nails that allow them to distribute the pressure of their weight in such a way that they can run over the water's surface or walk on floating vegetation. The ability to walk on the lily pads, and other vegetation, allows them access to the many insects, mollusks and small fish that are found beneath or around the floating plants. Jacanas are also good swimmers and occasionally dive as well.

Jacanas nest in floating vegetation and, when the eggs or young are approached by humans or other animals perceived to be potential predators, the adult birds feign broken legs and pretend they cannot fly in order to divert danger. The jacanas are usually seen flying and feeding in pairs, though a single female will also accept two males as her mates and the threesome has no trouble walking about on the same lily pad.

Grebes, duck-looking but not duck-related, are common water birds seen around lily pads where they feed on small fish, mollusks and aquatic insects. They also have the strange habit of eating feathers they find floating on the surface. They are also known to eat their own feathers as well. It is thought that the feathers offer some kind of protection to the stomach, perhaps as a type of filter for animal parts that cannot be digested.

The pied-billed and least grebes are found in the Amazon Basin, and both are expert divers. The pied-billed grebe can even descend without making any apparent diving movements, and uses this ability to escape predators. Grebes can dive down to about 7 or 8 metres but they cannot stay underwater very long. They build their large buoyant nests amidst but not on floating vegetation. Only a part of the nest is emerged and most of it is soaked. The eggs, however, are laid above the waterline.

Perhaps the strangest-looking bird seen near floating meadows is the horned screamer. This species looks like a cross between a chicken and a vulture with an antenna planted on its head. Its evolutionary relationship to other bird groups is unclear, though it shares some anatomical features with the ducks and geese, but superficially does not really look like any of them. In the Amazon the horned screamer is found mostly in the floodplain areas of the muddy water rivers where aquatic herbaceous plants are abundant. It is particularly loud – hence the name – because of the trumpeting calls it makes both on the ground and when on the wing. It is very fond of water hyacinth, especially young leaves, but also feeds on other aquatic plants including some of the grasses. When floodplain lakes shrink during the low water season, and the production of aquatic plants is greatly reduced, the horned screamers migrate to other areas.

When not feeding, horned screamers rest in the tops of trees and from a distance can be mistaken for vultures. Between the skin and the body is a spongy system of air spaces which is connected to the lungs. This, combined with very long wings, allows the horned screamers to fly to great heights. They often soar in large circles and so high up that they seem mere specks to the observer on the ground.

Horned screamers form breeding pairs and both the male and female, each caressing the other's head with its beak, appear highly enamoured during the mating season. They construct their semi-buoyant nests, next to or in floating meadows, from aquatic plant leaves and stems. The parents take turns incubating the eggs but cover them when both are away from the nest. The adults have a pair of large spines, or spurs, where each wing joins the body. The armed wings are used to protect the nest against predators.

Hawks, eagles and kites patrol floating meadows where prey, such as frogs, small insectivorous birds, insects and spiders are abundant. Some of the kites, such as the slender-billed kite, feed heavily on the large mollusks that become common in the meadows. The kites swoop down and grab the snails with one or both feet. While still in flight a kite can remove the hatch, or operculum, covering the snail's opening. With the operculum removed the kite then pokes its beak inside the snail to cut the connective tissue to its soft body. Once the soft part is dislodged the shell is freed and falls into the water or on to the ground.

Both the emerged and submerged parts of floating plants provide food and breeding habitats for many vertebrate and invertebrate species. The submerged root zone of one square metre of floating meadow will usually support over 500 000 invertebrate individuals. These include many insect orders, especially in their aquatic larval stages, crustaceans, mollusks, various worm groups and aquatic arachnids (spider relatives). Very few of these animals, however, feed directly on the roots themselves. Rather, foodchains begin with animals that graze the fungi and bacteria and other organic matter attached to the submerged roots and stems. Because animal diversity and abundance is so great in the root zone, it is still not understood how the animals distribute themselves in relation to one another. These root zones are, by population density analogy, the Manhattans and downtown Tokyos of the Amazon world of nature.

Terrestrial insects are much more successful than their aquatic counterparts at grazing floating plants, though grasses in general are not heavily attacked. Perhaps the insects most commonly seen feeding on Amazonian floating plants are *Paullinia* grasshoppers. Feeding in the open makes the grasshoppers very vulnerable to predators, especially birds such as the jacanas and anis. When attacked the grasshoppers often take to the water for short distances and sometimes attempt to hide themselves underwater. This strategy, however, is less than fool-proof as fish species readily snatch them up. Several of the grasshopper species that feed on floating plants lay their eggs below the water surface on the underside parts of leaves, such as those of lily pads and water hyacinths, or inside the leaf stems. The grasshoppers born below water find their way rapidly to the surface and climb on to the emerged floating leaves.

Several weevil-like beetles feed on water hyacinth leaves. Occasionally there are local population explosions of these beetles and the floating meadows of water hyacinths become blackened with leaf predators. The dense populations of beetles also attract many birds from above and fish from below and it is perhaps these predators that control the beetle populations.

Few of the floating plants produce seeds that are of much importance to animals. The major exception is wild rice, a species that colonizes the lowest parts of the floodplain where aquatic grasses are found. Wild rice is often found mixed with other grasses, though it is also common to find very large natural pastures of it looking very much like cultivated fields. Amazonian wild rice sets seed towards the end of the annual floods. Ducks feed heavily on the mature but still attached seeds. When the seeds fall into the water, large schools of young characin fish have a feast before the onset of the low water period.

The Amazonian Lowlands have around 100 known frog species, and floating meadow in and along the floodplains is their richest habitat. During high water there is an average density of about one frog for every square metre of floating meadow. Around 15 frog species will be found on or around large floating meadows, and this diversity contributes a disproportionately large part of the orchestra of animal calls that fills the nocturnal hours. Floating meadow frogs are almost exclusively nocturnal. Only one species, a *Lysapsus* frog, will sometimes call during the day, and then only when it is raining.

To frogs the floating meadows are like the orchestra stage of musicians where various instruments are segregated into special sections. The mating calls of individual species are very distinctive and easily distinguished not only by the frog but also by the human ear. Calling-site segregation with frogs is maintained by each species, or group of species, assuming positions on certain kinds of floating vegetation. Some species prefer very low vegetation with floating leaves only a few centimetres above the water. Others opt for taller grasses or the lower branches of flooded forest trees.

Few Amazonian frogs breed in open waters because of the presence of predatory fish. Likewise, few tadpole species are found in lakes and rivers, and the two species, both of the diverse genus *Hyla*, that are common in these types of waterbodies are endowed with toxins in their skins that discourage predation.

Several frog species found in floating meadows build nests made out of foam. These nests are initially formed by using the hind feet to whip up the mucus around the eggs with the surrounding water and air. Foam nests can be placed on land, on the water's surface or on plants. The tadpoles of *Adenomera* frogs have a large yolk-sac that enables them to undergo complete metamorphosis without the need to feed, thus the larvae do not need to enter the water. Other common foam-nest builders found in floating meadows belong to the *Leptodactylus* frogs. These amphibians build their nests on the water's surface, where there are spaces between floating vegetation or tiny pools. After metamorphosis the tadpoles swim away from the froth.

Hyla boans, one of the Amazonian frog species whose tadpoles readily enter open waterbodies, is also one of the most commonly heard amphibians in or along floating meadows. The males dig small depressions along the water's edge or sometimes in the thick mats of floating vegetation, and these holes then fill up with seepage water. The males call loudly from their nests to attract females. If other males attempt to intrude, the territory will be defended with the aid of curved spines at the base of the thumbs which are used as lacerating weapons. The eggs are attached to the water's surface, and the tadpoles develop downwards with the enlarged gills always in contact with water. Males often manage to attract several females, in which case eggs and larvae are found in various stages of development within the nest. The tadpoles are released by a rise in water level.

The *cururu*, as Amazonians call it, is the famous *Bufo marinus*, a toad that has been widely introduced in various parts of the world for attempted insect control, though it is native to the Amazon and other parts of South America. It is the largest frog found along Amazonian rivers and reaches about 20 centimetres in length. Of all the Amazonian frogs, the *cururu* is the most fecund, and a large female can lay up to 30 000 eggs though there is no elaborate nest building. The fertilized eggs and tadpoles are more or less left to the mercies of the environment. The eggs, however, do contain toxic substances in the jelly the female secretes around them, thus predation is greatly reduced. The *cururu* is one of the few frogs to take vegetable matter and carrion, and near human habitations it will sample almost anything edible.

The complex root mats of floating meadows are the home of some of the richest fish communities in the Amazon. Over 100 fish species can usually be found in a hectare of floating meadow, though this diversity decreases somewhat where grasses alone dominate because the root mats are then less complex structurally and probably also capture fewer nutrients. Root mats trap nutrients and much organic material washed in with the floods, and this sieving process greatly increases the growth of the floating meadows. The captured nutrients also lead to the development of communities of bacteria, fungi, algae and protozoans on which is based the foodchain in these habitats.

Few Amazonian fish species have evolved to feed directly on floating meadow leaves, stems or roots. For example, there is no Amazonian fish ecologically equivalent to the Chinese grass carp, an Asian species as its name indicates, that feeds heavily on aquatic herbaceous plants. The reasons for this are not clear, especially considering the fact the Amazon has the world's richest freshwater fish fauna with species that have evolved into about every feeding niche imaginable. Perhaps, as we will see later, the meadow-eating role is largely occupied by other animals.

Floating meadows add to Amazonian fish production more indirectly than directly, and this is through the detritus cycle. During the low water period the enormous quantity of floodplain herbaceous plants is left on the ground where it decomposes very rapidly because of high temperature and humidity. When the floods return the bottom layer is a thick and nutrient-rich organic mud built from the decomposition of the previous high water production of floating meadows. This organic mud is important in the diets of perhaps 100 fish species.

The largest detritus-feeding fish of Amazonian waters is the *cuiu-cuiu* (pronounced coo-you, coo-you) catfish, a species reaching over a metre in length and 20 kilogrammes in weight. Its outstanding features are the heavily armed flanks with bony spines and huge suction mouth. The heavily armoured fish looks like some Palaeozoic fossil that might have returned to life, though in fact it is a relatively modern fish whose body armour evolved independently of placoderms or any other ancient group that was endowed with outer bony plates. The giant fleshy lips of the *cuiu-cuiu* sit on a protruding snout that, when extended, forms an unbelievably large suction organ. The lip area is also endowed with thick barbels that the fish uses for navigation and probably food detection in the dark waters it works. The *cuiu-cuiu* vacuums up mostly the thick detritus that is enriched with bloodworms (certain types of fly larvae), tiny shrimp and other small animal life that lives in the organic ooze. Large populations of these fish are found in floodplain lakes where floating meadows are common, though of course the catfish are exploiting the previous year's production, now on the bottom and in a state of decomposition with the new floods.

The most abundant detritus-feeding fish is the *curimatá*, a silvery characin greatly resembling a carp. *Curimatá* live on very fine detritus that is often endowed with fungi, bacteria and algae. The detritus is removed with its suction mouth and processed by an intestinal system that is over 10 times the body length of the fish.

Floating meadows are extremely important nursery habitats for many fish species. Most of the floodplain fish species spawn at the beginning of the floods, thus their larvae are able to take advantage of the explosive growth of floating meadows that occurs at the same time. Fish larvae find both cover and plentiful food micro-organisms in these productive communities, though even in this habitat predation is still very heavy because of the wide range and large number of predators that have evolved to exploit fry.

Some of the most voracious of these predators are fish called *tucunaré*. *Tucunaré* resemble bass in general body form, but belong to the cichlid group of fish. The principal reason why *tucunaré* are so successful in Amazonian waters is that they are the only fish species of the region that are pursuit-predators. By pursuit is meant that once they attack they do not give up even if the prey is not captured during the first or second strike. Instead they continue their chase until usually capturing the prey, which is then swallowed whole. Nearly all other predatory fish will desist after a first or second unsuccessful strike.

The aquatic invertebrates of the root mats sustain not only larval fish but also a wide variety of adult forms. The floating meadows are the habitat where electric fish are most common. South American electric fish belong to five different families, but together they are often called knife-fish because of the shape of their bodies. Like the frogs that live above them in floating meadows, they are also nocturnal. Like frogs as well, they make a lot of noise at night, though this is done through electrical discharges rather than vocalizations.

Fish that possess cells, or groups of cells, sensitive to changes in electrical fields are relatively widespread in the world, and these include the rays, sharks, catfish and some others. Fish that can actually produce electricity are much less widespread, and in freshwater are only found in Africa and tropical America, though they have evolved quite independently. Several groups are able to produce powerful shocks, but in South America only the giant electric eel (500 or more volts) can do this. The other 70 or more species of South American electric fish produce only weak discharges in the range of millivolts to a few volts.

For the most part electric organs and electrical receptors can be used for two distinct purposes – navigation and communication. A third feature, paralysis, requires a powerful discharge and only the giant electric eel, mentioned above, has the generating potential for this. Electric organs have evolved from various muscle and nerve tissues and function in the following way. Cells are stacked and excited by spinal nerve signals in order to generate voltage. These stacks of electric cells are tightly surrounded by insulating tissues, thus the voltage contributions of the generated current increase just as in a series of small batteries connected together. Electrical receptors, on the other hand, have evolved from external nerve pits or lines along the fish's body.

Knife-fish have two kinds of electrical receptors. One type can respond to low frequency signals coming from electric fields other than their own. The second type can respond to the high frequency signals of the fish's own electrical discharge. Thus equipped, they can both locate and communicate electrically, which comes in very useful in the thick root mats.

Because knife-fish are common and almost constantly discharging their electrical organs, there is a lot of electrical activity in floating meadows. In fact, if you were to dip a listening device into the waters below a floating meadow at night, you could differentiate the buzzers and hummers of the electric fish world. The buzzers produce discharges as brief pulses, or clicks, separated by longer intervals. The hummers fire their electric organs in a more stable manner, so that when they are recorded on an oscillograph they appear as waves.

It is inviting to interpret the great variety of pulse and wave patterns generated by electric fish as specific communication languages within species. Ten to 20 knife-fish species are commonly found living in the same general area. For effective communication between the same species to be maintained, then each species must have at least slightly different peak frequencies in its electric organ discharge, just as each radio station must broadcast on a slightly different band length if jamming is not to occur.

The Amazon's largest animal is the manatee and its evolution in the giant river system is closely linked to floating meadows. Not including the Antarctic, the largest non-oceanic animals of all continents except South America are terrestrial. The American bison of North America and the elephants of Africa and Asia in part illustrate this point. South America, however, has no giant hoofed beasts. The continent's largest representatives are manatees, huge animals belonging to the sirenian group. Sirenians are so named because their body-form is reminiscent of the sea nymph Siren – part bird, part woman – of Greek and Roman mythology. Siren nymphs were said to lure sailors to death on rocky coasts by their seductive singing. Manatees have never sung to anyone, however, as they do not have vocal cords and, furthermore, they are extremely docile animals.

Adult Amazonian manatees weigh in at about 350–500 kilogrammes and reach 2–3 metres in length. The manatee body looks like a bloated cigar. Like the dolphins, but unlike any of the fish, manatees have a large, paddle-like tail that lies in a horizontal position and is moved up and down when the animal is swimming. The tail is an extremely strong paddle and can easily flip off two men standing on it. Manatees, interestingly, are thought to have evolved from the same ancestors as elephants. In water their bodies became more streamlined, necessitating the eventual degeneration of the hindlimbs, today only seen with the aid of X-rays as a vestigial pelvic girdle.

Amazonian manatees have extremely small and poorly developed eyes. They also have very tiny ears, but nevertheless their hearing is relatively good. Hearing seems to serve them best to detect the presence of Man, their main predator. Underwater their nose valves must be closed to prevent drowning, thus smell is apparently of little use to them. They seem to use taste buds on their tongues to recognize food plants and to pick up the scent of other individuals. The means by which they navigate through the dark waters underlying floating meadows is not understood.

Like elephants, manatees are non-ruminant herbivores, that is, they do not have compartmentalized stomach chambers where plant cellulose is fermented before digestion. Instead, fermentation takes place in the hind region of the digestive tract. In order to have enough digestive space and time to break down the tough grasses and other plants on which they feed, manatees have extremely long intestines equivalent to 20–30 times their own lengths. Because the plants on which they feed are generally poor in energy and nutrients they must consume huge quantities of them. A large adult manatee eats up to 50 kilogrammes of grass per day.

Manatees depend mostly on flowering plants for their diet. For marine species these are soft sea grasses, though they also feed on seaweed, or algae. The floating grasses and other aquatic plants found in Amazonian waters contain much silica, a mineral that helps to strengthen their anatomy in order to deal with oscillating water levels and perhaps also as a partial anti-herbivore defence mechanism. The teeth of the Amazonian manatee are literally 'filed' away by the silica in the plants it eats. To get around this problem manatees have tooth replacement, a feature that is not unique to them, though the manner in which they do it is not known in any other herbivorous groups. The molars are replaced horizontally, that is, the back teeth are constantly pushed forward until the front, worn elements are pushed out of the jawbone. Forward tooth movement takes place at a rate of about 1 millimetre per month, so that every 1–3 years the molars are completely replaced.

Manatees must feed heavily during the high water season when aquatic grasses and other plants are in abundance. They only rarely enter flooded forests, though they are known to feed occasionally on the leaves of *Cecropia* trees, which are also the favourite food of sloths. When waters fall back into the channels and floodplain lakes, the aquatic plants enter into a terrestrial phase and are out of reach of the manatees which cannot leave the water. During the floods, however, manatees build up huge fat reserves that tide them over during the 4–6 month low water season when food is scarce. Retreating to deeper floodplain lakes for greater protection, manatees largely fast until the new floods come and there is an explosion of aquatic grasses.

Manatees can stay underwater for about an hour before having to surface to breathe. One of their principal adaptations for long dives is a low metabolic rate, which means they need much less oxygen than, say, the dolphins which must surface much sooner. It is not inconceivable that hunting pressure in the last few centuries has caused a kind of artificial (man-induced) selection for animals that can hold their breath longest, as these would be the most likely to survive.

Amazonian manatees are probably polyandrous, with the female mating with several males. Manatees produce only one young at a time every two years after a gestation period of around a year. Since the young need to be born at a time when food is plentiful, mating takes place at the beginning of the floods so that the newborn will appear at the same time the following year. The young are only weaned after a year or more, though they may begin to feed on grass to some extent a few months after birth. Once grown, the manatees are essentially solitary, though small groups are probably common. Little is known about other social interactions.

Manatees not only eat a lot, but they also defecate and urinate to the tune of half the quantity of material that they ingest. A half-ton animal, then, during the high water season, returns about 25 kilogrammes of organic fertilizer to its environment every day. When manatees were abundant they were undoubtedly important fertilizers of Amazonian floodplain lakes since they 'unlocked', through eating and defecation, the nutrients that are contained within floating meadows. Today one can see this fertilization process taking place where water buffalo have been introduced into floodplain areas (unlike manatees, however, water buffalo trample and destroy many of the seedlings and saplings along floodplain edges and, within a few years of their introduction, radically change the ecology of the shores they inhabit).

Manatees had no major predators, if any, before Man. They protect themselves behind their thick hide and great body size. When Europeans arrived they found native Amazonians killing them for food, but there is no evidence for large-scale destruction by indigenous peoples. Europeans liked the taste of the greasy flesh, and the Portuguese soon named the largest animal of their newly-won kingdom the *peixe-boi*, or fish-cow. An open season, if not officially at least tacitly, was declared on the Amazonian manatee, and both the Dutch and Portuguese were involved. One observer noted that up to 20 Dutch ships stuffed with manatee were sent to Europe annually in the mid-1600s. A Portuguese Royal Fisheries station operating in the mid-1780s near Santarém at the meeting of the Tapajós and Amazon Rivers reported that approximately 1500 manatees had been killed in the area in a two-year period. Added to hunting pressure were the demands of the skin trade that operated heavily from the mid-1930s to the mid-1950s. With the improved tanning techniques developed at that time, manatee hides were turned into industrial belting, hosing and gaskets, not to mention glue. New synthetic materials developed by the mid-1950s largely destroyed the hide trade, but by then the Amazonian human population was increasing rapidly and urban markets were developing where manatee flesh could easily be sold. With the so-called 'economic development' of the Amazon beginning in about the mid-1960s, the commercial fishing fleets grew like a navy in preparation for war. By then manatee populations were too small to be hunted regularly on a commercial basis. However, the manatee is still hunted heavily because its size renders it one of the 'macho' animals on the masculinity-enhancement list of Amazonian fishermen and hunters.

Large grazing animals were at one time common in South America but most of them became extinct. For example, there were once grazing rodents the size of small horses. The principal grazer of the floating meadows along Amazonian river channels and floodplain lakes is also the world's largest living rodent, the capybara, an Amerindian name that means 'master of the grasses'. There is only one species and it is widespread in various habitats in South America. The nearest relatives to capybaras are the cavies, or as they are more generally called, the guinea pigs (also rodents), but the latter group is not common along Amazonian rivers.

The average capybara reaches about 50 kilogrammes and, seen from a distance in silhouette with the setting sun, it might at first be taken for a pig. One would first notice, however, that it does not have a tail and its front legs are shorter than the hindlimbs – no pig there. The eyes, ears and nostrils are set high on the head so that they are out of water when the animal swims. The partially-webbed feet act as small miniature paddles to propel the capybaras through the water.

Capybaras feed on a large number of aquatic grasses and floating plants and, like the manatee, lay down large fat reserves when food is abundant during the floods. Plant material is cut with the two pairs of large incisor teeth, then transferred to the molars where it is ground up before ingestion. They digest about 50 per cent of the grass material they eat as it passes through a long intestinal system. Along many Amazonian rivers, however, there are few aquatic plants because the water is too poor in nutrients to support them. Nevertheless capybaras are occasionally quite abundant in these areas, though little is known about what they feed on where aquatic plants are not common. In some rivers they feed mostly on submerged plants which they take while standing on the bottom, as do tapirs. Capybaras are also known to take the leaves of several tree species.

Smell is an important sense to capybaras. Males have a well developed oval-shaped scent gland on the top of their snouts that produces a white secretion somewhat reminiscent of diluted rubber latex. Both sexes possess a pair of glandular scent organs on either side of the anus. Those of the male contain detachable hairs coated with crystalline calcium salts. Females produce a greasy solution without the detachable hair feature. The chemicals produced in the anal scent glands are apparently different enough in proportions so that each animal in a group has a distinct smell and thus can be recognized by other individuals.

Amazonian capybaras breed at the beginning of the floods when food is plentiful. They mate in water where the male mounts the female, sometimes dunking her during sexual movements. Since the mating only lasts for a few seconds there is no danger of the female drowning. Gestation is about five months, thus the young – averaging about four per litter – are born before the end of the floods while aquatic plants are still available. The young are able to feed on grasses a week after birth. Capybaras reach reproductive maturity in about 18 months.

Capybaras live in relatively small groups of a dozen or so individuals consisting of a dominant male, several females and their offspring and subordinate males. A capybara day consists of heavy feeding during the late afternoon hours and at various periods during the night, followed by a morning rest and a midday bath to cool off if the weather is hot. When not feeding or bathing they sleep for short intervals. Some individuals are usually on the lookout for predators and, if spotted, they let out an alarm bark to warn the others, which then may rush to the water or sink into it if they are already there. Capybaras can hold their breath underwater for about five minutes.

Capybaras are now intensively hunted in most Amazonian floodplain areas. Molested and unmolested populations display quite different behaviour. Where Man is present and hunting capybaras, the animals tend to stay hidden in the nearby forest by day and only emerge at night to feed in the shore meadows.

Under natural circumstances, without the presence of Man, capybara populations are controlled by heavy predation on the young. Cats, caimans, snakes and some birds of prey are their natural enemies, though the first two groups have largely been decimated in floodplain areas. Unlike other predators, Man kills mostly adults or sub-adults, thus eliminating the breeding population.

It is perhaps appropriate to finish our exploration of floating meadows with a discussion of their most peculiar manifestation in the Amazonian river system. When the water level begins to drop rapidly, giant floating meadows are often towed by the currents into the main channel. Floating islands at least a kilometre long and several hundred metres wide are occasionally seen moving downstream. These often have small trees and shrubs growing on them whose roots have become established in the organic matter built up at the top. More spectacular, however, is their ark-like nature because of the large number of animals that are rafted downstream with them. Examining the root mats one will find the same fish and invertebrates that were found in the floodplains. Birds, such as anis and kiskidees, will chatter by day. Frogs will chorus at night. Sometimes larger animals, such as capybara, will also be aboard the downstream moving raft of life. Eventually the floating islands break apart and the animals disperse.

Amazonian waters are especially renowned for their predatory fish. The tucunaré (top) and red-bellied piranha (above and opposite) are among the most abundant predators.

Overleaf: During the low water period the flooded forests are drained. At this time beaches emerge in the river channels.

River banks are used by many different kinds of birds. The darter (top) perches in trees but dives to catch its principal prey – fish. Scarlet macaws (above) and many other birds use certain river banks as salt licks. The black-collared hawk (opposite) lives at the river's edge where it soars about in search of its main food – fish, crabs and mollusks.

The pirarucu *(top)* is the largest predatory fish of Amazonian floodplains. Cormorants *(above)* are the most abundant of the diving birds of the Amazon, their diet restricted almost exclusively to fish. The large number of predators has probably in large part been responsible for the evolution of specialized care of the young.

The arowhana fish (top) is a mouth-brooder and it is the male that protects the young. The fry are allowed out for brief feeding sessions, but are then soon gathered up into the protection of the cavernous mouth. Stingrays (above) are perhaps the most dangerous fish to Man in the Amazon because of the poisonous sting organ on their tails.

Previous page: Few animals are as highly adapted to live on beaches as is the black skimmer. The black skimmer is migratory and leaves the Amazon during the floods when beaches are submerged.

When water level falls and river banks emerge, butterflies flock to exposed areas that are rich in salts.

Overleaf: The giant pirarucu has traditionally been one of the most important food fish in the Amazon. It is taken with harpoons and gillnets.

◆ CHAPTER SIX ◆

THE

LAKES

AMAZON

The 'Rivers Amazon' is a term that has been used since the nineteenth-century naturalist, Henry Walter Bates, coined it in the title of one of the greatest natural history books ever written – *The Naturalist on the Rivers Amazon*. The term refers to the fact that the Amazon River is called three different names – Marañon, Solimões and Amazonas – and that the large basin is a land of rivers. There is, however, also a 'Lakes Amazon', a complex of thousands of open waterbodies that stud the floodplains of the Amazonian Lowlands.

Most of these lakes are filled on a seasonal basis with water that invades from the adjacent river channels. During high water one huge sheet of water sweeps from the river channels, over the levees, across the lakes, through the floating meadows and into the flooded forests. But when low water comes, the flooded forests are drained, the floating meadows are dumped on dry ground, the levees emerge and dam back the river channel waters from the floodplain. On the floodplains only the lakes are left, with little or no inundated forest and much reduced herbaceous plant communities. If a rainforest stream enters the floodplain, then a small channel through the levee to the river will be maintained. Otherwise, the floodplain lake is cut off from the river channel by the higher levees. Lake level, then, varies through seepage with low water river fluctuations.

At the end of the floods, as access to flooded forests is no longer possible and floating meadows disappear, most aquatic animals have two choices. To pass the low water period they can either migrate to the floodplain lakes or to the river channels (explored in the next chapter). Except for predators and some detritus-feeding animals, neither environment offers much food for the majority of animals.

Amazonian floodplain lakes, without their surrounding flooded forests or floating meadows, are not very productive habitats. Foodchains in lakes of nearly all kinds, and in oceans, are based on the production of phytoplankton, that is, algae found floating or drifting in the water. In general Amazonian lake water is too poor in nutrients or too muddy, or both, to support major foodchains based on plankton alone. This is why relatively few fish are found in the open waters of floodplain lakes during the high water period. During the low water period, however, fish and other animals are forced to take refuge in lake or channel if they are to survive. In the floodplain lakes most animals confront two major dangers, one physical, a lack of oxygen, and the other, a dense concentration of predators.

Most aquatic animals depend on dissolved oxygen in the water for their respiration. The amount of oxygen found in any particular waterbody depends on several factors. Tropical freshwaters in general are much more poorly oxygenated than those of the temperate latitudes where there is great seasonal variation in air temperature. Wherever there is a drastic drop in air temperature there is a corresponding fall in surface water temperature. Because water density increases inversely to temperature, cool water sinks, thus carrying with it a large amount of dissolved oxygen. Sinking cool water and the rise of the warmer water below to the surface is called turnover, and it is this process that largely explains the well-oxygenated waters of lakes and large rivers in cool climates.

In general water turnover, as mentioned above, is a good thing as it oxygenates the entire water column. In the Central Amazon, however, floodplain lake turnover often leads to the opposite effect. In late May and June, as the Earth is approaching the summer solstice of the northern hemisphere, cold Antarctic air is able to sweep northwards nearly to the equator. Cold fronts descending on the Amazon Basin usually last only 1–2 weeks, but air temperatures often drop below 15°C. The surface waters of floodplain lakes are chilled sufficiently to be cooler than the existing bottom layers, thus they sink to the bottom replacing them. The bottoms of floodplain lakes usually consist of a thick ooze of organic matter in some stage of decomposition. Within this ooze is trapped large quantities of methane gas, or hydrogen sulphide. This is easily seen when the bottom is stirred with a pole, as huge bubbles of methane gas will rise to the surface accompanied by an offensive smell. The Antarctic cold front, or *friagêm*, as it is called in Brazil, sends a charge of cool surface water to the bottom that in turn disturbs the 'locked' methane gas in the ooze layer. As the methane gas moves upwards and is dispersed in the water column it becomes a poison that interferes with the respiration of dissolved oxygen by fish, shrimp and crabs. These animals begin to appear at the surface in an attempt to skim the precious little uncontaminated dissolved oxygen that is found where the water and air meet. Nevertheless, huge numbers of fish and shrimp die and affected floodplain lakes turn into a fetid graveyard. Vultures by the thousands appear for what is for them a floodplain feast.

The Amazon system has at least 20 fish species that surface every so often to breathe atmospheric oxygen. It is usually believed that air-breathing species evolved during geological periods when there was a respiration crisis. These crises arose due to high annual temperatures, such as in much of the tropics today, and to the oxygen-consuming decay of dead organic matter that became trapped in the waterbodies, as happens in present-day Amazonian floodplain lakes. In this sense, many if not most Amazonian floodplain lakes must suffer, at least seasonally, a respiration crisis. The first known respiration crisis took place some 350 million years ago during the Devonian Period. It was at this time that the lungfish mentioned in the first chapter appeared.

Most Amazonian air-breathing fish live in a wide variety of habitats, most of which do not suffer deoxygenation. The South American lungfish, however, seems to be most content in oxygen-poor waters, or at least in waterbodies that suffer a depletion during the low water season. It is very seldom seen or captured in well-oxygenated streams or rivers. Its gills have so degenerated during evolution that they are now only vestiges of this organ associated with 'normal' fish. It indeed lives up to its name as it breathes with its lung. When floodplain waterbodies dry up, the lungfish, rather than migrate to other areas, entomb themselves in cocoon-like burrows in the mud, at which point they enter into a sort of suspended animation. Metabolic processes are turned down to the minimum to conserve energy until the new floods come and they re-emerge within minutes to feed heavily on fish, invertebrates and other prey on which they depend.

The *Synbranchus* swamp eels are another ancient group of air-breathing fish found in the Amazon, but also in much of South and Central America. They also have relatives in Africa and Southern Asia and travelled to the New World, along with the lungfish, on the South American geological plate when it separated from Africa. The swamp eel's respiratory solution – using the gills for both air-breathing and absorption of oxygen from the water – would seem to be ideal, though no other fish groups do this. The swamp eel also has a complex system of blood vessels in its mouth that can supply additional gas exchange between the blood and air. If oxygen levels are adequate, as during most of the flood season in the Amazon, the swamp eel does not surface to breathe. In the deoxygenated lakes and pools of the low water period, it surfaces, inflates its mouth and throat with air, then closes its mouth again to use the trapped air for respiration. If waterbodies dry up completely it burrows into the mud and can survive in a state of buried dormancy for several months.

The swamp eel's 'mouth lung' is quite rudimentary compared to that of the giant electric eel. Though both of these fish are commonly called eels, they are neither related to each other nor to any of the groups that also go by this name. The mouth might seem like a less than advantageous place for a lung to develop since it might easily be injured during food intake. Nevertheless, almost the entire mouth of the electric eel is lined with highly vascularized protuberances that provide sufficient surface area for oxygen uptake. The vestigial gills play no significant part in respiration, though they are still used to eliminate carbon dioxide.

The electric eel surfaces every few minutes for a gulp of air. Unlike the case with other air-breathing fish, however, oxygen is carried from the lung to the heart via veins instead of to the body tissues by way of arteries. Consequently, oxygenated and deoxygenated blood are mixed in the heart and this, much less than ideal, mixture is thus dispatched to the body tissues. It is because of this contaminated blood that the electric eel is unable to stay underwater for more than a few minutes.

With the mouth turned into a lung, the electric eel cannot afford to allow prey fish, many of which have sharp fin spines, to struggle too violently once captured. The electric eel gets around this problem by its ability to stun prey with potent electrical discharges in the range of 300–500 volts. In fact, the powerful discharge of the electric eel probably evolved more to protect the mouth-lung than as a defensive system, though it serves for the latter as well. Shocked prey are stunned long enough to be sucked instantly through the mouth and into the stomach before they have a chance to damage the electric eel's fragile oral lining. In some cases, however, the large predator does not stun its prey but, with lightning-fast striking speed, swallows the prey before it has any chance to struggle in the mouth cavity.

Several Amazonian catfish species are able to use their gastro-intestinal tract for air respiration. Portions of the gut of these catfish are thin and highly vascularized. Air is swallowed into the gut and oxygen is absorbed there. This system of air-respiration, however, is very inefficient because the circulatory system is such that oxygenated and deoxygenated blood are highly mixed in the arteries. As such, these fish must depend mostly on their gills but, when oxygen levels fall too low in the floodplain waterbodies, they supplement their respiration by gulping air at the surface. It is also unclear how these fish can breathe with their intestines when these organs are full of food, especially with the tightly packed detritus on which most of them feed. Air-breathing, however, is needed during the low water period when deoxygenation is most severe. It is suspected that the intestinal air-breathers feed heavily during the floods and fast during periods of low oxygen levels in order to leave the gastro-intestinal tract clear for respiratory purposes.

One of the two or three largest freshwater fish species in the world is the *pirarucu*, an air-breather, and it is perhaps the most appropriate ichthyological symbol of the Amazonian system, not only because of its size but also its great economic importance since the nineteenth century. Few accurate measurements of large *pirarucu* have as yet been made by scientists. The fish reaches at least 3 metres in length and 200 kilogrammes in weight, though heavy fishing now makes such large individuals rare. *Pirarucu* natural history, and perhaps even survival, is now so closely linked to Man that we will first consider the fisheries for this species.

In general the *pirarucu* was not an important food fish for Amazonian Indians. Without metal-tipped harpoons or, even more recently, gillnets, the *pirarucu* is a difficult fish to capture. The early naturalists to the Amazon found Indians taking mostly smaller fish, turtles and their eggs and manatees. Without salt, which was only introduced in any quantity with the European conquest of the Amazon, *pirarucu* is also a difficult fish to preserve. On the other hand, small fish can easily be captured when the need arises, turtles can be kept alive and manatee flesh was preserved in the animal's own fat rendered into oil. There was no need to try to capture the difficult *pirarucu* in any quantity.

The Portuguese who settled Brazil brought with them an insatiable taste for salted cod, a product that was imported from the homeland or from Scandinavian fisheries. By the nineteenth century the mixed cultures evolving in the towns and cities along the Amazon discovered that *pirarucu* could be substituted, at a much cheaper price, for the cod in the cuisine inherited from the Portuguese. The *pirarucu* even came to be called the Amazon cod (*bacalhão da Amazônia*). *Pirarucu* is exploited mostly during the low water period when it becomes concentrated in floodplain lakes. Though gillnets are being used today, traditionally the *pirarucu* was killed with steel-tipped harpoons when the large fish surfaced to breathe. This brings us back to one of the most amazing adaptations – air-breathing – of any Amazon floodplain predator.

The *pirarucu*'s air-bladder is quite different to that of most fish. In fact, the *pirarucu*'s air-bladder, thanks to the evolution of an interior system of blood vessels and its connection to circulatory plumbing, is highly reminiscent of the lung organ found in non-fish vertebrates. Though very different in structure to the typical vertebrate lung, the *pirarucu*'s air-bladder performs the same function, the intake of atmospheric oxygen and the elimination of carbon dioxide. Only very young *pirarucu* have functional gills, and these organs are used at most for a few days after birth, after which time the larvae surface to breathe. The gills then atrophy and are of no use. Adult *pirarucu* surface to breathe on average about every 10–15 minutes, though they can stay under for at least twice that long if need be, and especially when pursued by fishermen. The very young, however, must come to the surface every 4–7 minutes.

More than any other predatory fish the *pirarucu* is especially fond of deoxygenated waters and in fact seeks them out during the low water period because it knows instinctively that there will be an abundance of easy prey in these habitats. When oxygen levels are low, fish that have no special adaptations to breathe atmospheric air reduce their activity, and many even become torpid, in the floodplain lakes. This makes them easy prey for the *pirarucu*. Where *pirarucu* are still abundant, they can easily be seen and heard attacking fish near the surface as the latter search for precious oxygen.

Most predatory fish bite with their jaws, usually armed with teeth, and the *pirarucu* does this as well. The *pirarucu*, however, also has what is called a tongue-bite. Its tongue is very large and armed with teeth and, when pressed against the roof of the mouth, functions like a second set of jaws. Dried *pirarucu* tongues were traditionally used in the Amazon as seed-graters for making powder for soft drinks.

During the low water period the *pirarucu* builds up large fat reserves to provide the extra energy needed for breeding and for getting through the high water period when prey is widely dispersed in floating meadows and flooded forests.

When the river level begins to rise rapidly and waters are invading the floodplains, *pirarucu* now fat and adorned with bright red breeding colours form pairs in preparation for nest building and reproduction. At this time loud tail-slaps often accompany a rise to the surface to breathe. These noises may to some extent reinforce pair bonding or perhaps help frighten off potential predators of the young. Nest sites are usually chosen in shallow waters no more than 2 metres deep and amidst flooded vegetation, such as the guava shrub communities that often surround floodplain lakes, or in the more open areas of floating meadows as they begin to expand with the floods. Both the female and male, using their chins, fins and mouth, help gouge out a hole in the soft substrate. The completed nest might even be as much as 50 centimetres in diameter and 20 centimetres deep.

Unlike almost all other fish in the world, only the left ovary or testes is functional in the *pirarucu*. Interestingly as well, the gut passes to the left of the oesophagus and stomach, whereas in almost all other fish it is to the right. It is still unclear whether these two anatomical aspects are somehow functionally correlated. With only one ovary one might suspect that the *pirarucu* produced few eggs. After all, its nearest relatives, such as the arowanas, also with only one ovary, produce no more than about 200 eggs. At spawning time a large *pirarucu* has about 50 000 ripe eggs in its one ovary, and perhaps twice that many are undeveloped. All of the ripe eggs are deposited in the nest, at which time the male fertilizes them, and subsequently guards the nest. The female also stays in the general area to drive off egg and, later, larval predators. Still, predation is very heavy and only a few of the eggs or larvae survive the first few days in the nest. The eggs hatch in about 4–6 days, and by 6–7 days after that the young are ready to swim. By about the ninth day of life, the young begin to surface to breathe atmospheric air.

The young are dark in pigment and during the breeding and brooding period the adult male's head turns a matching greyish-black. The male swims about with its head lower than its tail. The newborn stick close to the dark head, against which they are well camouflaged. There are many reports that the very young feed on the thick head mucus of the male, though this habit has yet to be demonstrated scientifically. Because of heavy predation, not all of the young surface at once to breathe. Rather, smaller groups surface at intervals of about 60–85 seconds, thus decreasing the chances of the entire brood being eaten if predators are nearby. Once the young are large enough to fend for themselves they are abandoned and the male loses its dark head colouration.

Teeth are often literally at the cutting edge of evolution. The piranhas and pacus are closely related fish, very similar in general external characteristics and representing one of the greatest ecological divergences known in evolutionary history – one that is based mostly on relatively subtle changes in dentition. The piranhas, many species with almost razor-sharp teeth, have largely evolved towards predation, whereas the pacus with their blunter dentition have adopted a mostly vegetarian life. Because these fish evolved in tropical lowlands we have almost no fossil evidence of their origins and so no knowledge of which group appeared first.

Piranhas are a quite diverse group of fish found all the way from northern Argentina to Colombia. In the Amazon they reach their greatest diversity, with the group claiming at least 20 species. The most famous is the red-bellied piranha, the ignominious star of popular travel accounts and ichthyological horror films. If there is a dangerous piranha in the Amazon then it is the red-bellied species, though there are no verified reports of any human killed by these animals. There have been many injuries, but nearly all of these have been out of water when the piranhas were carelessly handled. During the low water period red-bellied piranhas can become very concentrated in the floodplain lakes of the muddy water rivers so danger is avoided by not swimming there.

The red-bellied piranha is the most blunt-snouted of its group and perhaps has the strongest jaws and sharpest teeth as well. It is adapted to bite out small pieces of flesh. Unlike most of its other kin in the Amazon, the red-bellied piranha is often a group hunter, at least during the low water period when populations of both predator and prey become dense in those floodplain lakes. Unlike the *pirarucu*, the piranhas will seek out the best oxygenated waters of the floodplain lakes.

Group size varies from about a dozen to perhaps over 100 individuals. Several groups, however, may converge in a feeding frenzy if a large prey animal is attacked, though this is rare. Piranha groups move about in search of prey concentrations and, once located, they appear to spread out like a battalion of soldiers dispersing to make ready for battle. Prey is usually ambushed by one or more of the group that act as scouts to pick out disadvantaged individuals. Once the prey is crippled one of the individuals will latch on to it, and this is the main signal to encourage the others to join in on the kill. They attack at lightning speed, each taking a bite or two and then darting out of the feeding frenzy. If an individual piranha becomes too gluttonous and continues to feed on the prey for too long others will bite at its fins to chase it off so that they can have a chance at the kill as well.

Most red-bellied piranha prey ranges from about half the predator's size to slightly larger than the fish itself. Medium-sized species are the main prey, principally because these are the most abundant. If the red-bellied piranha relied mostly on larger animals it would soon deplete its food resource. Larger animals are attacked, however, but these are mostly non-aquatic forms taken when swimming across the lakes. One red-bellied piranha population studied during the course of a year had attacked prehensile-tailed porcupines several times, apparently when these large rodents had descended flooded forest trees to disperse elsewhere in search of food. Occasionally red-bellied piranhas also eat relatively large quantities of filamentous algae, but the nutritional reasons for this have yet to be determined.

The voracious red-bellied piranhas are confined mostly to the floodplain lakes of the muddy rivers (e.g., Amazon and Madeira) where prey productivity is sufficient to support their large populations. They are only rarely found in any substantial numbers in blackwater and clearwater rivers, where they are replaced by other species, especially the black piranhas. There is a general rule for the distribution of Amazonian predatory piranhas: the poorer the water in fish productivity, the larger and more solitary the piranha.

Though the red-bellied and black species most closely fit the behavioural stereotype of piranhas as voracious predators, they are actually aberrant as most of the carnivorous species have evolved specialized habits that are more parasitical than predatory. There are around a dozen species of Amazonian piranhas that crop the fins or scales, or both, of other fish. These species seldom bite out pieces of body flesh. Fins and scales quickly grow back and thus represent a renewable resource. Also, fins and scales are high in protein, and the mucus on them contains valuable lipid fats as well. The fin- and scale-eating role is not a secondary one in Amazonian waters, but a major explanation of why so many piranha species can co-exist with each other, especially in the floodplain lakes during the low water period when they become very concentrated. If all piranha species were as highly predatory as the red-bellied and black piranhas, there would not be enough food.

It is highly probable that the fin- and scale-eating behaviour of piranhas first evolved with young fish. Piranhas in general undergo drastic changes as they develop, to such an extent that it is often very difficult to determine which young belong to which species. Young piranhas as a rule have very pointed snouts and this feature, along with sharp teeth, makes a highly effective fin-shearing tool and scale-removing device. Young piranhas, as with older individuals, do not appear to be very good at taking small fish. It is easier for the young to clip the fins and remove the scales of larger fish. The evolution of a species that retains the general shape and behaviour of the young of the species from which it split is known as neoteny. The fin- and scale-eating piranhas are probably in large part neotenous forms. In other words, the adults of these species have adapted to what was originally just juvenile behaviour.

The New World crocodilians are the crocodiles, alligators and caimans. Alligators are only found in the southern United States, whereas crocodiles live in all the major tropical regions plus the southern United States. Though crocodiles have been very successful in most of the major tropical river systems, they have not made it as far south as the Amazon Basin. In the Amazon the crocodiles are replaced by an ecologically similar group of reptiles, the caimans, or *jacarés* as they are called in Brazil. It is not at all clear why caimans are more adapted to the Amazon Basin than crocodiles would be, since the latter do well in other tropical river basins, such as the large Zaire system, but whatever the reasons they fill the same kind of niche.

Next to the giant anaconda the black caiman, or *jacaré-assu*, is the longest animal in Amazonian waters. Adults reaching 5–6 metres were probably once very common, though hunting pressure now largely prevents them from reaching this size. The black caiman was especially abundant in floodplain lakes and in the grassland swamps of the lower Amazonian islands, such as Marajó. During low water large numbers also migrated to sandbars along the rivers. Nineteenth-century travellers, bored with the tedious trip up Amazonian rivers, used to entertain themselves, according to travelogues of the period, by taking potshots at the basking reptiles. However, large-scale decimation did not begin until the twentieth century. Today the black caiman is most commonly seen in floodplain lakes during the low water period as it is too vulnerable to predation by Man if it moves on to sandbars along the river's edge.

With the introduction of lighting generators and other diesel-run engines in the first part of the twentieth century, there was a growing demand for precious oil in the Amazon. Diesel fuel often proved too expensive or difficult to import, and oil rendered from the caiman was used as a substitute, usually mixed in greater quantities with the former. The large-scale decimation of the black caiman, however, was due mostly to the skin trade that was spurred by the tanning industry beginning in the 1940s. Open season was declared on the black caiman, which was usually taken with a harpoon at night after shining a light in its eyes.

By the mid-1950s the black caiman had been largely killed off, and hunters started exploiting the smaller spectacled caiman. Caiman hunting for both skins and food continues today though it has long been illegal, at least on the books.

The most commonly seen crocodilian in the Amazon today is the spectacled caiman, so named because of the bony ridges around its eyes. Male spectacled caimans reach about 2.5 metres in length. The spectacled caiman lives in more or less the same habitats as the black caiman, as well as river banks swept by relatively fast-moving water, which the larger species usually avoids. Both species are hesitant to enter forest-covered streams, probably because the water temperature is too cool there, though they disperse throughout the flooded forest during high water. Whenever possible the black and spectacled caimans prefer warm water. By basking in sunlight for a few hours each day they can maintain body temperatures slightly warmer than those of the rivers and floodplain lakes they inhabit. These higher body temperatures mean that they need less energy, that is, food, to maintain themselves. At night, however, caiman body temperature is usually lower than that of Amazonian waters.

Both the black and spectacled caiman are gregarious animals, at least during the low water period in floodplain lakes and on sandbars and their beach waters. Where populations are still relatively large, it is not uncommon to see the two species mixed, especially near the inlets and outlets of floodplain lakes during the low water period when there are migrating fish. These caimans are best described as opportunistic carnivores, taking almost any animal food, alive or dead, that they can capture. Their foods include fish, birds, small mammals, larger crustaceans and mollusks, amphibians, insects and spiders. Caimans are among the few predators that feed on large toads, such as *Bufo marinus*, some of which have toxins in their skins poisonous to other animals.

The black and spectacled caimans breed in the water and nest on the land. Nesting takes place after the peak of the floods when the animals can be guaranteed dry sites around the edges of lakes and along river banks. Spectacled caimans appear to be more opportunistic nesters than the black caimans, and will breed almost any time from after the peak of the floods to the end of the low water period. Black caimans nest mostly during the low water months. Both species nest in relatively thick vegetation along the edge of quiet waterbodies and usually never very far from water.

The nest of the black caiman consists of a mound of tree leaves or herbaceous plant parts and can be about 1.5 metres in diameter and perhaps 50–80 centimetres in height. It is usually well camouflaged. The black caiman lays about 30–60 eggs which are deposited in two separate layers in the nest. The two layers are separated by a bed of rotting vegetation that, due to chemical reactions associated with decomposition, might help heat the nest chamber in some cases. Incubation time is to some extent determined by where the nests are located. If nests are exposed to warm sunlight the young can hatch in less than a month; in shaded areas incubation may take up to six weeks. Only the female guards the nest and she remains within distress call distance of her young.

The spectacled caiman constructs its nest at night from small pieces of woody and herbaceous vegetation and soft earth. The nest materials are first deposited in a large pile reaching about 1 metre across. The nest pile is hollowed out to receive the average 30 egg clutch. Incubation takes around 10 weeks.

Because of their large size (6–8 centimetres), caiman eggs make attractive food for a large number of predators. Prenatal mortality, especially because of egg predation, is 50–80 per cent. Egg and hatchling predators include the caimans themselves, anacondas, boa constrictors and other snakes, lizards, large cats, opossums and some of the larger wading birds.

The concentration of fish in the floodplain lakes during the low water period also attracts fish-eating birds. The shore zones are exploited by herons, egrets, ibises, storks and other wading birds that will be dealt with in a later chapter. The principal birds that are able to fish in the offshore waters are cormorants, darters, ospreys and various hawks.

The most common of the large fish-eating birds of the inland waters of the Amazon is the Neotropic cormorant, the only species of its group found in the region. Unlike other diving birds of the Amazon, cormorants are social and flocks with individuals numbering in the thousands are not unusual in some of the floodplain lakes where fish production is high. Judging by some of the bottom fish they commonly capture, they can dive to depths greater than 10 metres. They propel themselves with their greatly enlarged and webbed feet, and make highly dexterous turns in chase of prey by using the tail feathers as a rudder. Fish are grabbed with the beak, which has an anterior downward projection that helps prevent escape, and then quickly turned so that the prey is swallowed head first. Cormorants are fond of catfish, perhaps because they are often easier to capture, usually on the bottom, than mid-water fish. Catfish present something of a problem, however, because their dorsal and pectoral fin spines do not allow the prey to pass through the oesophagus. The cormorant gets around this obstacle by snapping the spines off with its beak, after which the prey is easily swallowed.

A feeding session can last up to an hour if prey is scarce and difficult to capture, though cormorants are reluctant to allow their wings to become waterlogged. After feeding they fly to beaches or to trees where they spread their wings to dry.

Cormorants make seasonal migrations in or across the Amazon Basin though little is yet known about their exact paths. The migrations appear to be related to nesting sites, as juvenile cormorants are relatively rare in most of the Amazon. Migrations through the Rio Madeira flightway, probably destined for the Eastern Bolivian Lowlands or Pantanal swamp area, often result in thousands of birds stopping off to feed in fish-rich lakes. When thousands of cormorants are roosting in the same trees, their production of faeces can actually kill the vegetation. On the other hand, they also defecate in the water while feeding and this undoubtedly helps fertilize floodplain lakes, a recycling process that adds to greater productivity.

One of the most aberrant forms of prey capture in Amazonian waters is stabbing. Darters roughly resemble cormorants though they have much longer necks, smaller heads and yellow bills, plus a huge fan-shaped tail. Occasionally darters are found amidst cormorant flocks but in general they are relatively solitary birds. They often swim or float about with only the head out of water. Their flying appears to be a precarious effort at best, and consists of flapping and sailing to travel relatively short distances. When not feeding they perch on branches above the water where they stretch their wings to dry, the same activity also serving to accumulate or dissipate heat depending on air temperatures.

Darters are slower swimmers than cormorants, but the snake-like neck can be shot forward with incredible speed to stab a prey animal with the greatly elongated and pointed beak. Once the prey is impaled, the beak is sometimes slightly opened to guarantee that the animal does not slip off and escape before it can be manoeuvred into the mouth. Darters attack fish, crustaceans and mollusks. They nest in trees above the water and usually in relatively open areas where they can see easily in all directions.

The fish-eating birds of prey are well represented in Amazonian floodplain lake areas. The three species most commonly seen are the osprey, common black hawk and black-collared hawk. All have long and curved claws adapted for grabbing slippery fish which they capture by plunging into the water, though only the legs and talons actually become submerged. The osprey is widely distributed in the world and most of the population found in the Amazon Basin migrates from North America during the latter's winter months. Nevertheless, a relatively large resident population remains in the Amazon Basin throughout the year, though the species does not breed in South America. Since the introduction and wide use of gillnets in the Amazon from about the mid-1960s, ospreys and fish-hawks sometimes accompany fishermen and patrol their fishing operations. When a fish becomes entangled in the top part of a gillnet the osprey and hawks will sometimes plunge down and try to remove it. Unfortunately, they sometimes get entangled in the gillnets too but fishermen are usually kind and remove them, as the birds command great admiration because of their fishing abilities.

CHAPTER SEVEN

PYRAMIDS

OF

PREDATION

Predators kill individuals but in the process promote the biological diversity of species. Intense predation pressure ensures that in most cases no one species will be able to increase its population to a point where it will dominate and eliminate most other species. This process aids species diversity and certainly in part explains why Amazonian waters are so rich in life, of both prey and predators alike. Predators, rather than physical factors such as high or low temperatures, poor oxygen levels and lack of space, account for about 80–90 per cent of the natural mortality of animals in Amazonian waters.

Each of the Amazon River system's major aquatic habitats has its characteristic top predators. A top predator is one which has few if any predators itself once it has attained a large size. Top predators are fewer in number than the prey they exploit because with each upward step in the food pyramid much of the food energy consumed by the animal is used for processes other than adding weight to its own body. These processes include movement, respiration, body temperature maintenance in some cases, waste elimination and reproduction. For example, a herbivorous fish may eat 15 kilogrammes of seeds for each kilogramme that it adds to its own body weight. A predator may need to eat 10 kilogrammes of herbivorous fish for each kilogramme it gains in weight. Thus, the energy needed for each kilogramme of a predator's weight is 'worth' 150 kilogrammes of seeds. Again, this is because so much plant energy has been lost through the physiological processes of both the herbivorous and carnivorous species. This concept is best visualized as an ecological pyramid. At the base of the pyramid is the plant source and the animals that feed on it, whereas the pinnacle consists of a much reduced number of predators.

No top predator has evolved to exploit all three of the Amazon River system's major aquatic habitats: river channels, floodplains and streams. Of the top predators only dolphins are common in both river channels and floodplain waters. Other than dolphins, the top predators in floodplains are the giant *pirarucu* fish (discussed in the last chapter), caimans and the anaconda. The last three are rarely seen in river channels, though caimans and the anaconda are found along banks and beaches as will be seen in the next chapter.

River channels have by far the largest populations of top predators of all Amazonian waters. Certainly the most abundant are the large catfish, though the dolphins, which have very high metabolic rates and hence eat a lot more, consume much more energy, that is prey fish, than their numbers alone might suggest. In terms of energy consumed, a 50-kilogramme dolphin probably eats at least 20–30 times more prey than does a 50-kilogramme catfish.

River level fluctuation is the main factor that explains why there are so many top predators in the running waters of the channels. River channel waters for the most part are too poor in production to sustain the large number of predators found in them. Most prey production takes place during the high water period in the floodplain waterbodies because of an abundance of flooded forests and floating meadows that form the base of the food pyramid (foodchain). But during the low water period, and during their spawning and dispersal migrations, the prey species enter the river channels in enormous quantities either to take refuge or to disperse to other areas. What these migrations represent is a flow of energy, via the prey fish, from the floodplains to the river channels. Much of this energy ends up in the stomachs of the top predators.

The most voracious and intelligent predators in Amazonian waters, the dolphins, have also been the model for some of the most interesting river folklore. Amazonian peasants generally know that dolphins are mammals, though they often refer to them as fish. A combination of the obvious intelligence of dolphins and their habit of constantly investigating any human activity on or in the water has served to stimulate myths about them. It appears that the rich folklore concerning Amazonian dolphins was derived mostly from the river peasant cultures that developed after the European conquest of the region.

Dolphins are often reputed to be the natural lifeguards of Amazonian rivers, and will not hesitate, according to folklore, to push a drowning person to shore. Less apocryphal perhaps is the claim that dolphins can be semi-trained to act as fishing partners. Dolphins regularly follow fishermen in the hope of taking advantage of discarded catches or to pick off fish fleeing from nets and other devices. Gig-fishing and cast-netting are common peasant techniques to which dolphins are attracted. A gig is a type of pronged spear that is used to stab fish, especially at night in shallow waters. The cast net is a hand-held net, thrown so that it opens in mid-air and lands on the water in an open position, at which point the lead-weighted peripheral line quickly sinks it to the bottom. Fish become entangled in the mesh as the net sinks. Gig and cast-net fishermen paddle slowly along near the shore. Some fish are frightened off and retreat to slightly deeper waters where the dolphins then attack them. Likewise, the dolphins frighten offshore fish into swimming in the direction of the fishermen.

The large-scale introduction of gillnets into the Amazon, however, has considerably altered fishermen's opinions of dolphins. A gillnet is a net set upright in the water into which a fish swims and then becomes entangled either by its gills or fins. Dolphins are incredibly clever at removing fish from gillnets – it is evidently less work for them than pursuing fish. They quickly pick up on fishermen's behaviour and favourite fishing sites. Near small waterfront villages, for example, they will often appear in the early morning or mid-afternoon hours to wait for subsistence fishermen who tend to fish more or less the same hours every day and often in the same places. They will then follow the fishermen and wait for them to set their gillnets. When fish become entangled they move in to take what they consider their own catch. Fishermen, mostly in vain, try to scare them off by beating the water with their paddles. Only in a few areas have fishermen actually taken to killing dolphins because of their molestation of gillnet catches.

Much of the folklore involving dolphins deals with sex in one way or another. Amazonian peasants derived the so-called 'feast-need' from their Amerindian ancestors, and this activity provided social cohesion among the sparse populations spread out along the rivers. Feasts, of course, are an excellent way for boy to meet girl. But girl sometimes gets pregnant with no apparent explanation, that is, assumed husband-to-be. Families have been known to use dolphins as scapegoats. Dolphins are supposedly able to transform themselves into handsome men, go ashore and blend into the feast. Young ladies can then be seduced, unawares, and are then abandoned by the young rake who returns to a cetacean life rather than face a shotgun wedding!

Dolphins are divided into two groups. The river dolphins belong to a group of five species, four of which are confined to rivers and one of which is marine. River dolphins are only found in South America and Southern Asia, and they evolved from marine ancestors that were once widespread. The Amazonian species is variously called Amazon river dolphin, pink river dolphin, or *bôto* (its Brazilian Portuguese name). Pink river dolphins are not a distinct species, as is sometimes claimed, but rather only old, large individuals whose underlying pinkish pigments are more prominent than in younger individuals.

The Amazon river dolphin reaches about 2.5 metres in length and 150 kilogrammes in weight, and is the third largest predator in Amazonian waters, following the giant *pirarucu* fish and the *piraíba* catfish. Like other river dolphins, its anatomical features are primitive compared to the marine delphinid dolphins. Primitive, of course, only means that they resemble features of those found in fossils of species now long extinct, and not that they are any less useful than more evolved characteristics. Compared to our general image of a marine dolphin, the Amazon river dolphin has a very slender and long beak, though it is well armoured with numerous, somewhat pointed teeth. Its dorsal fin is no more than a low ridge, rather than the high, shark-like one found in marine dolphins. Its flippers are large and broad with a finger-like trace pattern to them. The mellon, or fleshy protuberance, on top of its head is quite large for a dolphin, but the eye below it is so small that degeneration is suggested, and the atrophy of the visual nerve verifies this. For dolphins in general, the *bôto* has a relatively small brain, though it is larger than those of any of the other freshwater species. Even with their relatively small brains, as a dolphin goes, they are still among the most intelligent animals in the Amazon.

Muddy river water, such as in the Amazon, Ganges, Indus, Yangtze and Fuchunjian rivers where freshwater dolphins are found, supposedly rendered vision more or less obsolete for these cetaceans, and disuse somehow led to the evolution of near-blindness or blindness. The Ganges and Indus dolphins no longer even have lenses in their eyes, apparently distinguishing only light and darkness, and the Amazon dolphin may be headed in that optical direction. Poor eyesight, however, is more than made up for by echo-location, that is, sonar. The sonar headquarters of the *bôto* are located in the large mellon on top of its head. The mellon consists of special sacs through which air is forced by muscular movements. The sounds emitted from the mellon travel through the water until colliding with an object, from which they are then reflected. A sound receiving system is built into both the mellon area and the jaw mandibles. Interestingly, the Amazon dolphin also has what is called, in radar avionics, a look-down ability. The inferior edge of the mandibles are also endowed with receivers, thus the animal is able to explore the waters below it to some extent. The sound images formed enable the dolphins to determine size, direction, density and speed of objects. Thus equipped, they are able to identify a large number of prey species. It would be extremely interesting to know how large and specific their acoustical species identification is, since many of the fish they feed on are often very similar in size and shape. Other than ultrasonic transmissions, Amazonian river dolphins also produce clicks and other verbalizations with the aid of the larynx, and some of these may be used for both echo-location and communication.

Unlike marine dolphins the neck vertebrae in river dolphins are not fused. This means, unlike their marine counterparts, they can move their heads easily from side to side, thus enabling them to cover, without turning the entire body, a 90° arc on either side of the beak. The non-fused cervical vertebrae, however, render the river dolphins poor jumpers as they would probably hurt their necks if they attempted the aerial acrobatics of the marine dolphins. At most no more than about half of the *bôto*'s body leaves the water during the 'surface-jumps'.

What the river dolphins might lack in jumping abilities they more than make up for by their highly moveable head and its associated echo-location organs. By moving the head from side-to-side, the *bôto* can explore a relatively large area of its environment is one sweep, without necessarily having to turn its entire body. This ability is especially useful in the Amazon because of the large number of objects in the water which might otherwise obstruct dolphin navigation. During the floods, for example, most of the fish migrate into the flooded forests, and the *bôto* follows them into this complex habitat, whereas the *tucuxi*, which is related to the marine dolphins, cannot move its head laterally very well and thus sticks to the open waters. In flooded forests and other types of vegetation, the *bôto* can sweep-probe its environment to navigate easily and to detect prey. A dolphin that can only echo-locate head-on would have a difficult time in the flooded forest environment.

The *bôto* is one of the top predators in Amazonian waters and it moves easily between river channel and floodplain lake. During the low water period, however, the largest dolphin populations are found in the river channels. It is the only predator that regularly attacks the large catfish. All of the large catfish are armed with heavy bony fin spines, and these are often serrated like a saw for further protection. This fin-spine armour shields them from all potential predators except dolphins. Catfish usually remain near the bottom except when migrating. To capture a catfish on the bottom the *bôto* turns upside down during its dive, at the same time forming an echo-location map of the bottom and the prey by moving its head back and forth. With extreme and almost unbelievable accuracy the dolphin strikes the fish's peduncle, that narrow region between the main body and tail. The prey's tail is either severed or nearly so, thus crippling the catfish and preventing any meaningful escape attempts. Pieces of the prey are then bitten off, and more than one dolphin often shares the same catfish.

It is still unclear to what extent the *bôtos* fish together in groups. Up to 20–40 individuals can be found near river mouths when fish schools are descending tributaries to enter the main rivers. Two to four dolphins can be seen attempting to 'corner' a singled out prey fish, but the general impression given is that each predator is only trying to get it before the other does. There is no evidence that once one dolphin is satisfied it continues to help the others corral fish.

Bôtos breed during the low water season and, because the gestation period lasts about 12 months, the young are also born during the low water period. Sexual relationships appear to be determined by male dominance, and they are probably monogamous. During low water, fish are easier to capture and the additional energy may be needed for lactation. It is not known how long *bôtos* lactate, but it is probably several months. Judging by size, the single calf may stay with the mother for a year or more. The mother shares prey with her young, and it also appears that other adult dolphins (perhaps only females) will also share captured fish with calves.

The Amazon *tucuxi* (pronounced approximately too-coo-she) belongs to the marine family (Delphinidae) of dolphins. It is the only member of its family that lives exclusively in freshwater and it is found only in the Amazon river system. Its nearest relative is the Guiana dolphin, a species widely distributed in the coastal region of South America but which rarely moves further upstream than the brackish water zone. These dolphins are an excellent example of two closely related species that maintain an almost total geographical and ecological separation, presumably to avoid any competition for limited resources.

The *tucuxi* reaches only about 50 kilogrammes in weight, less than a third of the size of a large *bôto*, and rarely exceeds 1.5 metres in length. This means there are at least eight other Amazon river predators larger than it. There are, however, none faster nor more graceful than the *tucuxi*. The *tucuxi*, like other dolphins in its family, is able to leap completely out of the water. It is not unusual to see three or four *tucuxis* leaping into the air together, and they are almost always in perfect formation so that they re-enter the water at the same time. These highly co-ordinated jumps are very reminiscent of the performances displayed by the marine species kept in animal parks. Like the *bôto*, the *tucuxi* has very poor eyesight and navigates mostly by echo-location.

Although the *tucuxi* is widespread in all types of Amazonian rivers, it has not been as successful in as many types of habitats as the *bôto*. It avoids the flooded forests and, whereas the *bôto* is occasionally found above cataracts, the *tucuxi* never is.

Dolphins feed mostly on fish and as most fish are in the *igapó* forests during the floods this would appear to pose a serious problem for the *tucuxi*. Like several large river predators, the *tucuxis* in fact probably pass several months of the high water season on a much reduced diet. It is still not known whether they also reduce their swimming activity at this time to conserve energy. Luckily for them, at about the mid-point of the floods and when water level begins to drop, enormous schools of characin fish begin to form and to move out of the flooded forests and down the clearwater and blackwater tributaries in order to migrate upstream in the muddy rivers such as the Amazon and Madeira. These high water migrations last for about three weeks, or until such time that the fish re-enter flooded forests. The large schools of fish in the swollen rivers offer a feast during the famine floods for the *tucuxi*. Subsequent to these migrations, the fish will remain in the flooded forests for another 2–3 months that is until the low water season comes and they are forced out into the floodplain lakes or river channels.

During the 6–7 months of each year when flooded forests are drained, many if not most fish species form large schools in the reduced waters to which they must retreat. The *tucuxi* dolphin is most often seen attacking pelagic fish, that is, species living in open water. It does not fish on the bottom like the larger *bôto*, and only rarely attacks large catfish.

Tucuxis, often in pairs, have the habit of leaping out of the water in pursuit of jumping fish. It is not unusual to see predator and prey airborne, though of course no more than about half a metre out of water. They also appear to jump into the middle of schools and on the downward descent pick out an individual prey to chase. Commercial fishermen often wait in tributary mouths for schools of descending fish. When *tucuxi* are spotted churning the water with their leaps, the fishermen prepare their nets for they have been 'advised' that a fish school is approaching.

Little is yet known about the breeding behaviour of the *tucuxi*. Most marine dolphins are promiscuous, so perhaps the *tucuxi* is as well. As mentioned, the *tucuxi* is certainly so in folklore. What we do know so far of *tucuxi* sex life is that the males have very large testes, often reaching 5 per cent of the animal's total weight (in humans it is less than $\frac{1}{4}$ of 1 per cent). It is thought that the female accepts various males from a breeding group that forms around her during her receptive period. It is not so much the males *per se* competing for the female, but rather their sperm within her. The more copious the production – that is, the larger the testes – the greater the chances of winning the fertilization contest.

The Andes, the Amazon and the Atlantic are an alliterative and geographical trio whose limits span nearly 5000 kilometres along a line of latitude. As described earlier, the geology of the Andes has literally been carried eastwards by water where it partly ends up as silt or dissolved nutrients in floodplains whose rivers have headwaters in the high mountains to the west. However, by far the greatest part of the silt and nutrients is not left behind but is carried downriver and eventually out into the Atlantic. As the muddy Amazon meets the Atlantic its current is sapped and there is much sedimentation of both inorganic matter and organic ooze.

The damming effect of the Atlantic leads to the decanting of the heavy sediment load carried by the Amazon. The improved water transparency, backed up by the rich nutrient base, leads to huge plankton blooms, especially of diatoms which are single-cell algae. There is also a rich organic layer on the bottom as a result of both sedimentation of detritus brought downriver and the rain of plankton produced locally. If there is any place in the Amazon River system that might be considered a nutrient gold mine, it is at the meeting of the Amazon and Atlantic. One of the Amazon's principal predators, the *dourada* catfish, long ago in its evolution discovered this wealth of productivity at the great 'meeting of the waters'. Ironically, *dourada* means 'the gilded one', named after the colour of the fish, but it is so ecologically appropriate as well as no other known animal's life history embraces the 'golden' opportunities offered by the Andes, the Amazon and the Atlantic.

The *dourada*, with its platinum head, gilded to yellowish body and long tailfin lobes, is one of the most beautiful catfish in the world. Its life history has also come to represent a sort of zoological search for 'El Dorado' – the mythological city of riches sought after by many explorers. In recent years as export catfish markets were opened, Amazonian commercial fishermen went in search of the *dourada*, of which they knew very little before these operations began.

To follow *dourada* life history, and much of the mystery still associated with it, we must begin with the larvae and young. During the high water period the Amazon actually pushes the Atlantic somewhat oceanward, thus forming a larger area where the combination of Andean nutrients, increased transparencies and the sedimentation of organic matter build highly productive foodchains. It is at this time of year that newborn *dourada* appear, and it is as if they were dumped from above in these productive waters, as breeding schools have yet to be discovered by commercial fishermen or anyone else. Fishing effort is very intensive in the waters around the island of Marajó and, though thousands of tons of *dourada* are captured, ripe fish are never among these.

In the rich Andean nutrient-fed waters around Marajó, young *dourada* grow rapidly on a diet of shrimp and fish. When they reach about 50–75 centimetres in length, they begin to move upstream in large schools during the low water period, a time when marine water invades further inland because of the reduced discharge of the Amazon. These young predators, then, are recruited from the lower Amazon into the inland waters, where they join larger individuals of their own species that have migrated in previous years. It is not known how far upstream the young recruits migrate in the first year after they leave the lower Amazon. Older populations in the rivers appear to disperse over wide areas of river channels. There they feed heavily on the characins and catfish (other than their own species) that become concentrated during the low water period and at the beginning of the floods when spawning migrations take place. *Dourada* can be seen following and feeding on the schools of migratory characins as they make their way upstream.

Unlike most predatory catfish that hunt only at night, the *dourada* feeds both nocturnally and diurnally, at least when prey is abundant. Also, unlike most predatory catfish, it has very short barbels, thus it cannot do much 'feeling around' in the muddy waters in which it mostly lives. It evidently relies heavily on its vision.

It is perhaps the *dourada*'s unique colouration that helps it capture many of the fish on which it feeds. Its silvery head is approximately the same size and reflects light in water in about the same way as its silvery prey. So, the prey mistakes the head for another fish of its own kind, or is even attracted to it as a kind of lure. The golden to yellowish body behind the predator's head is well camou-flaged in muddy water. The *dourada* is also unlike other large predatory catfish in the Amazon in that it uses the entire water column, from the surface to 30–50 metre depths, for feeding. The other large catfish feed mostly on the bottom or near it, where they find their way with their large barbels.

At the beginning of the floods huge schools of *dourada* begin to migrate upstream in the central and western Amazon. The average fish in these schools is about 75 centimetres to 1 metre in length. Nowhere are these migrations more spectacular than at the Teotônio rapids of the upper Rio Madeira near Porto Velho in the southern Amazon state of Rondônia. By late December the Rio Madeira has risen about 8–10 metres from its minimum low water point three months previously. The charge of floodwaters from the Bolivian Andes that is ushered down the Rio Madeira is squeezed between the high banks of the Teotônio cataracts. The rapids themselves, studded with huge slabs of resistant granite rock that churn the rushing water as if in a cauldron, present about a 10 metre drop between the smooth water above and below the cataracts. When the schools of *dourada* reach the Teotônio cataracts, they violently fight their way up the rapids, using the 1–2 metres near the shores where the current meets its greatest resistance because of frictional drag on the bottom. Fishermen, perched on scaffolding overhanging the rocks, gaff the catfish as they negotiate the tur-bulent waters.

The Rio Madeira schools of *dourada* are known to migrate to near the base of the Andes in the Eastern Bolivian Lowlands. It is more than 4000 kilometres from the Amazon mouth area, where the *dourada* are born, to the Andes, via the Rio Madeira. The fish probably take 2–3 years to migrate this far upstream. At some point in their lives, the *dourada* must migrate back downstream in order to breed in the highly productive waters near the mouth of the Amazon river. These downstream migrations occur during the floods to take advantage of swift currents in the middle of the rivers. Very few of these ripe fish are captured because of the difficulty of fishing in mid-river where huge quantities of wood, fallen trees and herbaceous plants are transported downstream during the floods. Ripe fish are over 1.2 metres long and 20 kilogrammes in weight. Since newborn *dourada* are found towards the end of the floods, it is possible that ready-to-breed catfish moving downstream to the Amazon mouth area are able to migrate 4000 kilometres or more in 1–2 months. After all, water falling in the Bolivian Andes, transported down the Rio Madeira at an average flow of approximately 1.5–2.5 metres per second, takes at most about a month to reach the Atlantic. Riding the river water downstream the *dourada* use relatively little energy getting back to their breeding grounds after a long period of feeding in the inland waters. It is highly possible that they spawn in the main channel of the Amazon, just upriver of the large island of Marajó, where the current has yet to be broken by the Atlantic, and where the newborn will be carried downstream and spread widely in the highly productive waters of the estuarine area.

It is not uncommon in the Amazon for young and adult fish, as with the *dourada*, to be ecologically and geographically separated. This appears to be especially true for some of the species that are the most abundant. These ecological separations have probably evolved to reduce both interspecific (between species) and intraspecific (between size classes of the same species) competition for limited food resources. The *dourada* has taken this strategy to the limits, making its home range nearly the entire Amazonian Lowlands from the Atlantic to the Andes.

The *piraíba* (pronounced peer-ah-ee-bah) catfish, reaching about 3 metres in length and around 200 kilogrammes in weight, is the largest animal of Amazonian river channels. Of Amazonian animals, only the manatee is larger and it is found mostly in floodplain waterbodies – habitats that large *piraíba* do not enter. The *piraíba* lives mostly on or near the bottom of river channels, and is captured on long lines at the 30–50-metre depths common in some of the deeper Amazonian waters. The giant catfish is perhaps one of the few species that regularly descends below 30 metres, though most individuals appear to live in 10–30-metre waters. The *piraíba* is most active nocturnally, at which time it moves into shore waters to capture its prey fish. The giant catfish has three main feeding periods during the course of the year. During the low water period, prey retreating from the shrinking floodplains become concentrated in the river channels where they are heavily attacked by the *piraíba*. At the beginning of the floods when the water level rises very rapidly, *piraíbas* migrate to tributary mouths to wait for fish schools descending to spawn in the main muddy rivers such as the Amazon and Madeira. For a month or so at the beginning of the floods, various species of spawning fish are in abundance, but once the breeding season has ended the *piraíba* finds little food in the river channels for 3–4 months. The large predator reappears again at river mouths after the peak of the floods when schools of characin fish begin to migrate from one tributary to another further upstream.

The barbels (whiskers) of the *piraíba*, as with many catfish species, are sensitive to touch and probably to smell as well. The predator, thus equipped, can both feel and smell the presence of prey in the dirty and dark waters it hunts at night. It can also hear them, as it has a well-developed inner ear connected to its sound-receiving air-bladder. In fact, many of the prey, on which it feeds heavily, produce sounds, thus betraying their presence to this large predator. The *piraíba*'s eyes are so diminutive that vision, in the muddy waters where the predator is most common, is probably of very limited use. The giant catfish also possesses a pair of organs located behind the pectoral fins that produce a creamy, latex-like solution. This solution is sometimes discharged when the catfish are captured. Fishermen folklore claims that this *piraíba* 'milk' is used to nurse the newborn, but much more likely it is a type of pheromone, that is, a chemical released into the water to transmit some kind of smell signal about aggression, territoriality or breeding. In other words, pheromones improve communication in dirty waters where vision is of little use in picking up behavioural signals. Feeling, smelling and listening are the senses by which the giant predator finds its way in its light-deficient habitat.

No Atlantic fish species has evolved to spawn in Amazonian river waters and likewise none is known to migrate from the freshwater environment to the sea to breed. The absence of Amazon-Atlantic migratory animals is probably due to the relatively little time, geologically speaking, that the two great waterbodies have been in contact. At best the Atlantic can offer up only wanderers that make their way into the Amazon, though most of these do not go beyond the point where the tides are still strongly felt, that is, about 200 kilometres from the ocean.

The two largest oceanic wanderers into the Amazon River are the bullshark and the sawfish. It is highly unlikely that either one of these species has evolved physiological adaptations specifically for living in fresh as well as saltwater, as in neither case do their life histories depend on any phase in rivers. The bullshark, nevertheless, when entering rivers is able to reduce the urea (nitrogen) content in the body fluids by 30–50 per cent. If it could not do this, its body would absorb dangerously high levels of water and become bloated (in principle, just as salt absorbs water in a humid environment). Furthermore, rectal glands that are used to excrete excess salt in marine waters stop functioning when the species enters freshwater, and the urine becomes more copious and dilute.

Bullsharks wander especially far up the Amazon, in fact they nearly reach the Andes some 5000 kilometres upstream. Sawfish do not appear to wander so far, though they are known 2000–3000 kilometres from the Atlantic in the Amazon river system. These large fish are seldom captured outside the main Amazon River channel, and there are no verified reports of them in clearwater or blackwater rivers, perhaps because prey is too scarce in these nutrient-poor tributáries.

Both bullsharks and sawfish are abundant in the estuary, but neither is able to maintain large populations upriver. In some of the Central American river-lake systems, especially in Nicaragua, bullsharks and sawfish are among the most important predators. Their relatively poor showing in Amazonian waters is probably due to the presence of other large predators, especially the giant catfish and dolphins, that out-compete them for food. In general bullsharks and sawfish appear to be opportunistic and are only abundant in freshwaters where there are no other large predators to compete with them.

The largest bullsharks and sawfish entering Amazonian waters reach about

2.5 metres in length. Though bullsharks the world over account for most of the recorded shark attacks on Man, they are so seldom seen in the Amazon as to be of no real concern to bathers.

The top predators in streams and smaller rivers, especially those running through rainforest shade, are quite different from those of the larger river channels. In fact there is very little overlap between stream and river channel predators, and they probably only come into contact with each other near the confluence areas that sometimes spread out to form swamps.

Otters are the top predators of Amazonian streams, though today this is very difficult to see because these mammals have been so heavily hunted. The giant otter is appropriately named as it is the largest member of its twelve species group. From head to tail it can reach about 1.8 metres and a weight in excess of 30 kilogrammes. Of animals commonly found in Amazonian streams, only the anaconda snake is larger. Giant otters usually live in small groups of about 3–8 individuals. In areas of small rivers where fish become concentrated during the low water period, groups of 10–20 individuals may form, though today these are only found in protected areas because of hunting pressure.

During high water when fish disperse, the larger otter groups break up into smaller units. Normally, an otter group consists of an adult pair and one or two litters that establish a territory along a stretch of stream.

Giant otters are very vocal, even in the presence of humans. A repertoire of no less than nine distinct sounds has been recorded. Scent marking is also an important means of communication. Freshwater otters have a pair of scent glands near the base of the tail, and these organs are responsible for their musky smell. In addition to marking territories, scent can communicate such information as sex, numbers of individuals in a group and sexual receptivity. Territories are also delineated with faeces and urine markings.

The giant otter is the least terrestrial of the otters. This is reflected in its extremely large and highly webbed feet which make it somewhat clumsy on land. The paddle-like feet along with an extremely streamlined body make it a very fast swimmer. Prey is chased underwater and captured with the mouth. Brought to the surface, the prey is then manipulated with the hands so that pieces can be bitten off and swallowed.

Amazonian streams, like the rivers into which they flow, change drastically during the course of a year. During the floods, streams are dammed back by river waters, thus inundating the surrounding forests. It is probably in this habitat that otters fish during the flooding season, as few fish remain in the streams themselves. Otters do not appear to enter the huge floodplains, or at least not on a large scale. Rather, they stay near streams, and perhaps this is due to their need to define territories and to have dens along the bank to which they retreat at night. Otters have dens distributed throughout their home range. The den they inhabit at any particular time depends on water level and food abundance.

Like other large predators of Amazonian waters, otters probably have a more difficult time feeding during the floods than the low water season when fish become concentrated. It is still not known if otters time births to coincide with fish abundance, though this is to be expected. The gestation period of giant otters is only about 70 days, thus they could begin breeding as soon as food is plentiful and also give birth when fish are still concentrated during the low water period. The young are born in a selected river bank den, often with a submerged entrance for greater protection.

The Neotropical river otter is even less well known than the giant otter, though it is much more widely distributed and embraces several races in Central and South America. It is only half the size of the giant otter. Smaller size allows the Neotropical river otter to live in shallower waters than the giant otter and, though it has been too decimated to detect its distribution patterns accurately, it appears to have been even more oriented to headwaters than the giant otter.

Only two marsupials have evolved for an aquatic life, and both are found in the American tropics. Ironically, Australia has a much more diverse marsupial fauna, but none of the species has become aquatic. Of the two, only the water opossum, or *quica* or yapok, is found in the Amazon river system, the other species being restricted to mostly non-forested areas. The water opossum is a small animal, reaching only about 30 centimetres in total length from head to end of tail. Like the otters, it lives mostly in small streams, though its secretive habits make it more difficult to see. With its mottled fur, it is one of the most attractive of the American opossums.

Like otters, water opossums have large, webbed hindfeet ideal for swimming. Water opossums are more hand-oriented than otters, at least in prey capture. Whereas otters tuck their forelimbs backwards against their bodies while swimming, and use only their mouths for capturing prey, water opossums swim with the forelimbs extended forwards to feel about the environment and grab prey. They also make much use of their whiskers to sense water movements, which makes prey capture easier. They undoubtedly feed on smaller fish than the otters and thus do not enter into competition with them.

Surprisingly both male and female water opossums have pouches. During a dive the young are protected in the mother's watertight chamber. The O-ring and lubricant combination used to protect underwater mechanical equipment, such as video camera housings, is based on the same principle as found in the water opossum's pouch. Instead of a rubber O-ring and petroleum jelly, the water opossum uses long hairs around the lips of the pouch and an oily secretion to form a seal. The seal is tightened down when strong sphincter muscles pull the pouch closed before a dive. The male apparently finds it necessary to protect his scrotum when swimming and can withdraw it into his pouch if need be.

The dwarf and smooth-fronted caimans – reaching maximum lengths of 2.2 and 1.5 metres respectively – are a closely related species pair that are usually found in rainforest streams, small rivers or habitats where the black and specta- cled caimans are missing or relatively rare. Unlike the other Amazonian caiman species, the smooth-fronted caiman does not bask in sunlight. This is perhaps a reflection of the fact that it is more adapted to live in the cool, rainforest-shaded stream waters. The dwarf and smooth-fronted caimans, unlike the two larger species living in floodplain lakes and along rivers, are mostly solitary and tend to avoid open areas. During the day they often stay hidden under sunken logs or streamside vegetation.

Prey production in and along streams is too low to allow large numbers of caimans to live together and still feed themselves. Moreover, in order to survive in streams or small rivers the dwarf and smooth-fronted caimans must feed on a wide range of prey animals, and they apparently take almost any invertebrate, especially large insects and spiders, and vertebrates small enough to be killed. Their vertebrate food includes fish, frogs, water birds, small rodents and occasionally other caimans.

The smaller caimans nest along the streams where they live and, like the larger species, construct egg chambers mostly of plant matter and earth. Their nests can be about 1.5 metres in diameter and perhaps half a metre in height and they are constructed in such a way that air temperature inside is about 4°C higher than the surrounding environment. The dwarf caiman produces about 13–18 eggs, whereas the smooth-fronted caiman lays only 10–13 eggs, both spe- cies considerably less fecund than the larger pair found in open waterbodies. Incubation appears to take at least three months. It is unclear whether the female guards the nest and it is probably not to be expected considering the long incu- bation period. Newborn dwarf and smooth-fronted caimans do not race to the water, but rather spend several days near their nests while the mucous layer cov- ering their skin dries up. They are extremely vulnerable to predation during this period, especially as the nests are apparently unattended by adults. The very young of both these species have ochre to nearly red coloured heads. This char- acteristic is somewhat reminiscent of several of the Amazonian turtle species whose young also have brightly coloured heads. The purpose of the bright head colours in these reptile groups is not known.

The most voracious fish found in Amazonian rainforest streams are the *traíras*. These fish are characins somewhat resembling a black or grey-mottled tube with the anterior part full of teeth. The *traíra* body can slide easily under leaves or logs, and this is where these fish like to hide by day. They have very large eyes and are the owls of the aquatic world of Amazonian rainforest streams. Subsequent to the rainy season, rainforest streams become packed with a large supply of fish, many of which have migrated into these habitats from the river channels or floodplains. As the dry season progresses and the streams diminish in size, the prey slowly disappears, that is, it is eaten by the *traíras* and some close relatives also found in these habitats. At the end of the dry season, the fish in a rainforest stream pool might be over 90 per cent *traíras* in weight. When otters were still common, this was probably much less the case because one of their favourite fish prey is the *traíra*. The otters helped maintain higher fish diversity in streams by keeping *traíra* populations reduced.

CHAPTER EIGHT

BEACHES
AND
BANKS

The riverbeds of the Amazonian Lowlands are blanketed with sands and silts that have been transported downstream from the headwaters. The large fluctuations in water level each year are seasonal tides that ebb and flow across tens of thousands of kilometres of beach habitat where the sands and silts have been piled up at the river's edge or around islands. During the high water period the beaches are drowned in at least 5–12 metres of water and this causes migration of the animal communities which have developed in the shallower waters during the low water period, or on the sandy shores. In general, beach development in the Amazonian Lowlands is extensive for about 4–7 months each year. Perhaps about one half of the total shoreline found in the large rivers of the Amazonian Lowlands consists of beaches during the lowest water months. River islands greatly add to shoreline development and most are surrounded by beaches. The other half of the river channel shoreline consists of alluvial or upland banks that are covered with vegetation.

Beach life can be very diverse aquatically, but terrestrially the number of animal species is greatly reduced due to the lack of cover and high surface temperatures during the day. In beach waters fish are by far the most diverse and abundant vertebrates as the habitat is an important low water refuge for many species. Caimans were at one time also common, but today, because of their destruction, very rare is the beach that has large numbers of these reptiles. The most common reptiles found seasonally in beach waters and on the emerged sands are turtles. Snakes are seldom seen on beaches or in their waters, though the anaconda will move into beach pools cut off from the main river and where a large quantity of prey fish often becomes trapped. Frogs are also rare on beaches for lack of cover. Man is now the only mammalian predator to stalk Amazonian beaches, though folklore claims that the jaguar and some of the smaller cats attacked turtles in times long past. Many bird species occasionally land on beaches or along the shores, though only a few are highly adapted to use this habitat to any great extent.

The first turtles, as fossils indicate, could not withdraw the head into the shell and thus were vulnerable to predators. As predation pressure increased there was selection for greater protection, and species evolved that could withdraw the head into the shell. Most living turtles in the world retract the neck in a vertical plane so that the head is still pointing forward when it is withdrawn. This allows the animal head protection and the widest angle of vision considering the position of its eyes beneath the overhanging upper shell (carapace). However, the other main stock of turtles, to which most Amazonian species belong, took a different route in cervical evolution, and retract their necks horizontally, that is, to the side. These are the side-necked turtles, and they are largely restricted to an aquatic life. Life on land would be dangerous for them since the front limbs interfere with complete withdrawal of the neck and head, thus exposing these vulnerable parts to terrestrial predators.

The side-necked turtles have spread far and wide in the Amazonian river system, perhaps because they have been there for such a long time. They have either replaced most other turtle groups or prevented them from entering the large river system during the course of geological history.

One species that has probably been using beaches since the Mesozoic Era is the giant Amazon river turtle, the *tartaruga*. The *tartaruga* reaches over a metre in length and 75 kilogrammes in weight. If the Amazon river turtle could have somehow known that Man would eventually become its major predator, it certainly would not have evolved to nest gregariously on beaches. Of over a dozen species of Amazon river turtles, only the *tartaruga*, the largest species, deviates from the standard pattern which is for dispersed and individual nesting. The *tartaruga*, like the giant marine turtles, migrates in large numbers to specific beaches to lay its eggs in the sand.

Traditionally the *tartaruga* was exploited mostly on beaches during the nesting period because this is the only habitat where it is relatively easy to capture. During the floods it retreats to flooded forest to feed on fruits and seeds. When the Portuguese and Spaniards arrived in the Amazon Basin they found the native tribes capturing large numbers of the *tartaruga* during the low water periods. No one knows for sure whether the native tribes consciously developed management and conservation practices for the prized food animal but, whatever was the case, the large turtle was very abundant when the first Europeans arrived.

Missionaries and traders became as interested in the eggs as in the turtle meat, for the eggs could be rendered into cooking and lighting oil. The native peoples had not previously made extensive use of the eggs for oil and apparently only dug out of the sand those that would be eaten. Turtle egg oil was prepared by crushing thousands of eggs in a canoe and then flooding it so that the yolk-fat would come to the surface. The oily mixture was then skimmed off and placed in large kettles for purification and reduction. The final product was stored in clay pots. In the mid-nineteenth century, the naturalist Henry Walter Bates reported that a turtle oil pot required about 6000 eggs to fill it. He calculated that in the Upper Amazon and Madeira region alone at least 48 million eggs were destroyed yearly. This represented the fruitless nesting of some 400 000 female *tartarugas*.

As the mixed Amazonian cultures evolved in the last two to three centuries, the *tartaruga* in the local cuisine was elevated to an almost mystical level. No other food animal is so highly regarded – for eating that is, not conservation. Today the large river turtle is too rare to serve as a major food animal, but it is nevertheless intensively exploited in the illegal game trade. The *tartaruga* is considered a must, if at all possible, for birthdays, weddings and other celebrations and the upper classes pay very high prices to obtain the large turtle. This encourages hunters and fishermen to go to great lengths to capture them, since a single large *tartaruga* can fetch as much in the illegal game market as would normally be earned in 2–3 months.

If we look at beach development during the low water period in the Amazon today, there does not seem to be any lack of nesting space, so why does the large *tartaruga* form nesting groups as large as 7000 individuals and restrict laying to relatively small areas?

Man preys mostly on *tartaruga* adults and their eggs, whereas fish, caimans, snakes, birds and dolphins attack the young after they hatch and descend the beaches to the water. The only reasonable explanation of why the river turtles evolved to nest gregariously is that their large size prevents them from using the more diverse habitats of the smaller species. Furthermore, during past geological times beach sites were much more limited than at present, especially when sea levels, hence river levels, were higher. It is still unclear, however, whether the large turtles migrate *en masse* to the nesting sites or, perhaps more likely, join numbers there from various converging upstream and downstream populations that have an imprinted or memorized navigational 'fix' on the reproductive site.

As the rivers reach their low water ebb, the large turtles begin to gather in the deeper waters near the beach sites where they will nest. This phase can last several weeks, until the turtles are sure that water level has reached its minimum, at which time they begin to move into shallower waters with their heads usually facing towards the beach, in periscope fashion. Eventually they move on to the exposed beaches. They then sunbathe and apparently also take temperature and humidity readings by rubbing their heads against the sand or lifting their heads high in the air as if to smell it. This behaviour may last several days to a couple of weeks, during which time they may return to the water before night falls. Egg-laying may be nocturnal or diurnal, though the former is probably more common, especially with the advent of Man as predator.

Once on the beach and ready to nest, the large river turtle excavates a hole in the sand where the eggs will be laid. The hole can be up to a metre deep and 0.5 metre diameter. The nest chamber itself, however, is only about a fourth of that size. Excavation, egg-laying and egg-burial can take up to four hours to complete, though it is normally done in 2–3 hours. The average clutch size is slightly less than 100 eggs, but up to 180 eggs can be laid by larger individuals. Incubation takes around 45 days.

Man is probably the only major egg-predator, as other animals have a hard time finding and excavating the relatively deep chambers. The hatchlings emerge in two distinct waves, usually at night, and this strategy perhaps evolved to double their chances of survival, since the first wave usually consists of only about 60 per cent of the clutch. The remaining newborn clamber out 2–3 days later. Once out of the nest the young turtles must race to the water through a predatory gauntlet. The simultaneous appearance of huge numbers of young was perhaps the principal strategy that the large Amazonian turtle used to guarantee its survival in face of the great number of predators that the young must face.

The major bird species that use Amazonian sandy beaches extensively are all migratory. The annual floods literally expel beach birds and they must move elsewhere. There is no known case of bird migration between sandy beach and adjacent forest. The adaptations needed to live along sandy beaches are in general unsatisfactory for an arboreal life. Also, the beach birds need dry land on which to roost and thus cannot spend the high water months floating about. Wading birds, such as some of the herons and egrets, are occasionally seen in sandy beach areas, but they much prefer shallow floodplain waters, vegetated shores or mud-flats where it is easier for them to catch prey and where they find more appropriate perching sites in the trees.

Little is yet known about the exact migratory routes of the birds that seasonally enter the Amazon Basin. Perhaps the bird that comes from furthest away is the lesser golden plover. It migrates all the way from northern Canada and Alaska, though its main winter range is not in the Amazon Basin but mostly in the southern Brazilian and Argentinean area. There is probably too much competition for limited seed and insect resources from a variety of other Amazonian birds, and perhaps too many predators as well, for golden plovers to stay in larger numbers in the open habitats of the Amazon. Nevertheless, they are commonly seen on Amazonian beaches and some populations are resident for a few months each year. The lesser golden plover usually arrives in August or September at about the same time as beaches are emerging in the Central Amazon. By January or February the plovers begin to migrate northwards and reach North America in March or April and then breed in the summer months in the northernmost latitudes.

Two other types of plover, the southern lapwing and pied lapwing, are more commonly seen on Amazonian beaches than the lesser golden plover. Unlike the last species, the former two do not migrate from North America. Instead, their migrations are confined to the tropical region and, beyond that, southward into southern South America. The southern lapwing is found on Amazonian beaches in groups of usually around 10 or more individuals, but sometimes as many as 100 birds. The pied lapwing, on the other hand, is solitary or found in pairs. Both species feed on insects, mollusks, crustaceans and to some extent small fish found along the shore. They excavate small holes in the beach sands for their nests. If alarmed by potential predators they let out a consistent series of 'keks' that warns others, including other species as well. If a potential predator gets too close they fake being wounded to divert it from the nest. When the floods come adult and young alike migrate, apparently mostly south.

One of the most interesting birds to watch along Amazon beaches is the black skimmer. It is especially unique because it is the only bird whose mandible (lower beak) is much longer than its maxilla (upper beak). The skimmer's lower beak is so elongated that the bird cannot pick up objects from the ground. The beak is only useful in the water. The skimmer flies close enough to the water so that its long lower beak skims just beneath the surface. When its prey, which is mostly small fish, crabs and shrimp, is touched, the head is bent down slightly and the beak is closed. Occasionally it will also fall from the air in a somewhat spiralling descent to snatch up its prey. It fishes mostly at dusk and at night. During the day it rests on beaches where it can easily see the approach of potential predators for hundreds of metres.

Black skimmers build their nests on Amazonian beaches just after the sands emerge at the end of the flooding season. The nest is no more than a shallow hole where 2–3 eggs are laid. If danger appears the adults fly along the water's surface to inspect the situation though they are usually not very threatening to intruders. As terns are better at diverting or expelling intruders that is probably why black skimmers often nest near to them on Amazonian beaches.

The large-billed and yellowed-billed terns are found on the beaches of most Amazonian rivers. They fly at much reduced speed along the beaches during the day in search of fish and other prey. When a prey animal is spotted they flap their wings and descend vertically, sometimes diving down to about a metre's depth. When turtles are hatching, which is usually when the river level is rising and just starting to inundate the lower parts of the beaches, the terns form what is perhaps their largest concentrations on the interior waters of the Amazon. As the young hatchlings emerge from their buried nests and race towards the water,

Floating meadows are made up mostly of grasses that grow upwards with the floods. The Pipa toad (above) is one of the few Amazonian frogs that is entirely aquatic. It protects itself from predators by remaining hidden beneath leaves or in dense vegetation during the day, emerging only at night to feed on small fish and insects.

Overleaf: Floating meadows, unlike the flooded forest, decline during the low water season. During the floods, however, they are very productive habitats and provide much cover and food for many animal species.

The spectacled caiman (above and opposite).
At one time caimans were extremely
abundant in the Amazon. Today they are in
need of protection because of over-
exploitation.

The manatee (top) is the largest animal of Amazonian waters. It has been intensively hunted for food and is now extinct in many rivers. The capybara (above) is one of the few terrestrial animals that feeds heavily on the plants of the floating meadows of the Amazon.

The anaconda (top) is one of the commonest, but most difficult to see, predators along Amazonian rivers. Although large, it is able to remain hidden in floating meadows or underneath leaves. Giant otters (above) were at one time common in Amazonian streams and smaller rivers but, like the manatee and caimans, they have been over-hunted.

Previous page: One of the most spectacular fishing sites in all of the Amazon is at the Teotonio rapids of the upper Rio Madeira. Fishermen perch themselves on scaffolding in order to gaff fish migrating upstream.

The Lower Amazon is the richest wading bird region of the Amazon. Among the most beautiful of the wading birds are the spoonbill (top) and the scarlet ibis (above and opposite).

The floodplain of the Lower Amazon has been deforested in many places. Giant water lilies do well in this region because of shallower waters.

The most voracious of the large predators in Amazonian waters are dolphins. The bôto dolphin (top) regularly enters flooded forests, whereas the tucuxi dolphin (above) stays mostly in river channels and floodplain lakes.

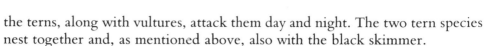

the terns, along with vultures, attack them day and night. The two tern species nest together and, as mentioned above, also with the black skimmer.

Beaches are extremely important habitats for a large number of fish species during the low water period. A large beach, in fact, will normally have more fish species than are found in all of the freshwaters of the British Isles. The average Amazonian beach will be visited by 50–100 fish species during the low water season. Many species appear to prefer beaches to floodplain lakes, and in general these are the fish with excellent vision or ones adapted to feed on the small invertebrates found in sand. Most of the beach species, with the exception of predators, form relatively large schools. During the day hours, these schools move slightly offshore and remain deep enough, usually below about 2 metres, so that they are below the zone of light penetration. As dusk approaches, however, they move into the shallower waters for better protection against the large number of predatory catfish that feed at night. Schooling also reduces predation because the predators have a more difficult time attacking a prey when it is surrounded by a large number of other individuals of the same species. The predator has a difficult time focusing on and following an individual when it is part of a school.

There is little food in most sandy beach waters except for predators and the species that can sift through the sand to remove algae and invertebrates. In general, for non-predatory species, the food found in beach waters is probably secondary to that found during the floods in floating meadows or in the flooded forests. On the other hand, the many different predators have a feast.

The largest predatory fish found in shallow beach waters are the stingrays. Several of the species reach over a metre in diameter and 30 kilogrammes in weight. All of the species have a venom apparatus called the sting which is usually well serrated so that when injected the victim receives not only venom but also a serious wound. The sting response is only elicited for defensive purposes, and then only when pressure is felt against the disk-like body. It is never used to capture prey. The tail is whipped forwards in a curve with the sting pointing to the area of body contact. The sting easily penetrates rubber boots and is powerful enough to be driven into wood. Stingrays cover themselves in sand and most accidents occur when they are stepped on in beach waters. Leg, ankle and foot scars caused by stingrays are common among fishermen and Amazonian peasants living along rivers. Initial pain is extreme and is usually accompanied by spasms, cramps and cursing. Death from stingray injections is very rare, but intense pain can last up to 10 days, and full healing may take from 1–5 months. Local treatments, given the lack of proper medical attention, are of dubious value, but include rubbing tobacco juice on the wound to urinating on the foot. Apparently the opposite sex is required for full potency of the latter prescription.

Stingrays are ovoviviparous, that is, the eggs are fertilized and developed within the female. The males have large claspers that they use to fasten on to the females in order to intromit their sperm. The developing young stay within the female for several months, during most of which time they are transparent. The young are most commonly seen when stingrays are captured and the females abort.

Amazonian stingrays probably feed mostly at night when they move into shallow beach waters where they can pounce on small fish and crabs. They excavate holes and cover themselves in the sand of shallow beach waters and their abundance is easily verified by observing the round depressions they leave after abandoning a site. As water levels rise or fall, stingray holes are the deepest spots just along the water's edge. Though only a few centimetres deep, the depressions are nevertheless used by many small fish moving into water too shallow for larger predators. Stingrays, then, are important micro-habitat builders for many small fish inhabiting Amazonian beach waters.

Another species that hides in sand is the electric sandfish. When night falls electric sandfish rise, or rather they 'pop out' of the sand of shallow waters where they remain hidden during the day. The largest sandfish reach about 30 centimetres in length, though most are less than 20 centimetres. They are nearly transparent and this factor, along with their light colouring, makes them well camouflaged against the sands where they are usually found. After emerging 25–40 minutes after sunset the sandfish forage along the bottom for tiny insect larvae which they are able to remove from the sand with tubular snouts. They have no teeth and prey are sucked out of their hiding places.

The electrical discharge of the electric sandfish is very weak, and in fact it can only be detected with the use of special instruments. While foraging, sandfish are electrically very active, producing bursts of around 200 hertz. Sometime between about 3 and 5 a.m. they burrow into the sand. The sand is entered head-first, and against the current so that there is a downstream drift of particles which facilitates the burrowing. The burrowing process only takes about half a second, thus decreasing the chances that a predator will see where the sandfish is hidden. If need be, however, the sandfish travels about under the sand to flee danger. Once buried in the sand, the sandfish reduces its electric discharge to a mere 10–15 hertz, but why the organ needs to fire at all during rest is unclear. Perhaps the low discharge helps to establish territories, especially during the burrowing hours of early morning.

The communities of fish that move from the floodplains to the river channels, and then to refuge in beach waters, include a large number of predators, which themselves are also vulnerable to even larger predators such as the channel catfish and dolphins. Two groups of predators with dog-like, or canine, teeth are especially abundant in beach waters, though they are also common in floodplain lakes as well during the low water period.

The dog-tooth characins (family Cynodontidae) have a pair of huge fang-like teeth in the lower jaw. These teeth are so large that two holes in the upper part of the head are needed to accommodate them when the mouth is closed. Some of the dog-tooth characins reach nearly a metre in length. The dog-tooth characins attack relatively large prey, usually elongated fish that can easily be pulled through the mouth and forced into the voluminous stomach. The prey fish is sometimes 40–50 per cent of the predator's own length. The prey is first stabbed with the pair of huge canine teeth, which in many cases punctures its air-bladder, thus rendering it helpless. It is not unusual for the stabbing teeth to be driven completely through the prey as they are sunk into it with such force.

Two groups of predatory fish common on beaches resemble arrows. These are the needlefish and the so called pike-characins (family Ctenoluciidae). These fish have pincer-like jaws used to grab small fish and insects near the water's surface. They often attack obliquely, in which case they bend their bodies, just like a bow, to build up the tension that will shoot them, with the speed of an arrow, at their prey target. The pike-characins are especially interesting because they have a bright to almost metallic red, or orange, fleshy appendage on the end of the upper part of their beak-jaw. This appendage is often poked a little out of the water in which case it attracts insects. Small fish are also attracted to the brightly coloured beak. The upper beak, then, is apparently a lure to attract various kinds of insect and fish prey.

Parasitic fish are also very abundant in beach waters, especially the scale-eaters. Certainly one of the most obnoxious ones, at least to the scaled fish, is the *Roeboides* group. These characins have conical teeth on the inside of their mouths but also nipple-shaped teeth, or protuberances, on the outside part of the jaws. The *Roeboides* fish will ram or butt a scaled fish to dislodge its scales. They will usually then circle about the fish they have attacked and snatch up the sinking scales. Looking closely at a *Roeboides* school one will notice an accompanying related characin mimic that is about the same size and has the same general markings. The one main difference is that it lacks the outer, nipple-shaped teeth. The mimic, a *Charax* fish, has very small scales thus it does not have to fear attack from the *Roeboides*. The scale-eaters, however, probably offer it protection from many predators – at least the scaled ones – since they avoid getting too close to schools of *Roeboides*.

Most of river banks of the Amazonian Lowlands are levees, that is, ridges of sand or clay that accompany the channels. The levees are built from the larger alluvial particles, as these are the heaviest materials in suspension and thus the first to be deposited when river levels rise and invade the floodplains. Because of deposition processes, levees are usually the highest parts of the floodplain and the last strips to become completely inundated. Under natural circumstances the levees are covered mostly by trees and shrubs that are the riverward edge of the flooded forest. Where levee deforestation has been extensive, such as along much of the Amazon River, Humboldt's willow tree, a colonizer, forms linear stands on the soft alluvial soils. The lower banks of muddy rivers usually support tough cane grasses that, as discussed earlier, grow up with the floods. During the low water period the new growth reaches about 1–2 metres and forms a verdant herbaceous aspect to the levees. The levee banks of the clearwater and blackwater rivers are usually devoid of herbaceous plants but support a rich shrub flora.

No birds are more associated with the river's edge than kingfishers. In the world's largest and most complex river system, which also contains the richest freshwater fish fauna, kingfishers would appear the most likely avian candidates to benefit from the seemingly endless amount of shoreline that is bordered by forest. The kingfishers are, in fact, a relatively large group of birds but their centre of greatest diversity is the Old, not the New, World. The Earth's largest river can only claim five of the world's 87 kingfisher species. Because the riverbank forests, and the birds in them, were not isolated from one another over large areas during the Ice Age dry periods, kingfishers were not compressed into smaller areas that might have led to greater species divergence in this group. All five species of kingfisher found in the Amazon are widely distributed in South and Central America.

Kingfishers catch their prey by diving from overhanging branches or diving from the air. They usually return to a good fishing perch, within their home range, in the early morning or late afternoon hours, until the spot no longer proves rewarding. Surprisingly, most kingfishers do not fish inside the flooded forest despite the large number of potential perch sites available. Light conditions within the flooded forests are generally too poor for kingfishers to locate and effectively dive on their prey. The green-and-rufous kingfisher, a solitary species that keeps low, has made the greatest incursion into the flooded forest. Even there, however, it prefers open, though shaded, areas along streams, including those cutting through the levees and connecting floodplain lakes with the rivers. Fish use the levee streams for moving back and forth between river and lake and, due to the great amount of overhanging vegetation on which to perch, all kingfishers do well in these habitats.

Kingfishers are undoubtedly the commonest of the widely distributed fish-eating birds in the Amazon as a whole. They form the only group of diving birds that has done well in the extremely nutrient-poor blackwater and clearwater rivers. Other diving birds, such as cormorants and darters, require areas of greater fish production, such as the floodplain lakes along the Amazon River, to build up populations of any size. Kingfishers prefer waters that are relatively clear and smooth, as turbidity and waves interfere with their search for fish and crustaceans. If fishing becomes difficult they will attack flying insects.

All diving birds that descend from the air on their aquatic prey must deal with refraction, that is, the bending of light as it passes obliquely from one medium (air) to another (water) of different density. For example, when standing on the bank and looking at a fish in the water, what one is really seeing is not the exact location of the animal, but rather its 'bent' image as a result of the refraction of light. If the fish were co-operative enough and would not move, you could easily prove that what you see is not the fish but its refracted image. If you reached into the water at the point where you see the fish's image, you would soon discover your mistake. Kingfishers and many other diving birds possess two foveae in the retina of each eye – one central, which is the common pattern for most vertebrates, and one that is lateral. The fovea is the rodless region of the retina where vision is most acute. This double fovea provides the diving bird with both monocular and binocular focusing and is therefore just what is needed to correct refraction distortions and pinpoint the whereabouts of the fish before the dive.

Of the more than 160 species of snakes found in the Amazon, relatively few are aquatic or semi-aquatic. Snakes in general are not very good aquatic predators compared to fish. The habitat where Amazonian snakes are probably most abundant is along the river, floodplain or stream banks. This is due to the concentration of prey, much of which comes down to the edge at night to water or to feed. Eight different groups of snakes are found in Amazonian waters or near their edge. Of these, only the coral snakes and vipers are venomous. The vast majority of snakes are not poisonous.

The most famous snake of Amazonian river banks and the shallower waters associated with them is the anaconda. There are reliable measurements of anacondas 10 metres in length. Since it is much heavier, this makes it considerably larger than the world's second largest snake, the python of Africa. There are also 2–3 species of smaller anacondas that seldom exceed 3–4 metres in length. Anacondas are now probably the most abundant predatory reptiles on many Amazonian floodplains. Caimans were at one time more abundant than anacondas but they have been greatly decimated through hunting.

Anacondas feed on a wide variety of aquatic and terrestrial shore animals. In the water they take fish, small turtles, caimans and wading and diving birds. Along the shore they capture rodents, especially the capybara, small deer, tapirs, peccaries and other ground mammals. It is unclear how much they hunt in trees, though they are commonly seen on branches in the flooded forest, or emerging from the holes of hollow trunks. Anacondas are most active at night but also hunt during the day. They do not chase prey but rather move to spots where animals are watering or feeding and then ambush them. A large animal is grabbed by the neck, and almost instantly the anaconda coils around it. Constricting not only immobilizes and kills the prey but in many cases also crushes it into a softer form so that digestion by the snake is easier. Smaller prey are grabbed and killed with the mouth and teeth alone. The head of the prey is swallowed first and ingestion of the entire animal takes place slowly as the victim is pulled backwards through the mouth with the teeth. The anterior part of the lower jaws have a very flexible articulation and at the back they are only loosely connected to the skull. Thus, the lower jaw can be greatly distended to allow large prey to be pulled through the mouth. Prey killed along the shore is often dragged into shallow water, perhaps because an anaconda with a large prey animal only half way ingested would be very vulnerable to attack from jaguars. Also, both predator and prey often become very covered with biting or stinging ants during the kill period, and the eyes and nostrils are especially vulnerable. By moving into the water both the predator and its dead prey can be freed of vicious ants.

It is not known how often anacondas feed in the wild but, like many other Amazonian predators, they perhaps build up fat reserves during the low water period when prey is more concentrated along the water's edges. In captivity they can go for months without a meal.

Anacondas, like most other Amazonian aquatic reptiles, mate in the water. Gestation is about the same as for humans, that is, nine months. Anacondas are ovoviparous (young born alive) and litters that have been counted ranged between 14–82 individuals. The newborn are about 75 centimetres in length. They reach 3 metres in length by their third year.

There are reports of anacondas attacking small children, but most of these are probably exaggerated. In the last century, the reliable Henry Walter Bates reported two cases in which anacondas had wrapped around children, but the toddlers were rescued before constriction killed them. Anacondas are most often killed not because of any serious threat to humans, but because they attack floodplain farm animals, such as pigs, chickens, ducks and dogs.

Boa constrictors are nearly always presented as the terrestrial counterpart to the semi-aquatic anaconda and in large part they are. Boa constrictors, however, are often common in or along Amazonian waters. They reach a maximum length of about 4 metres, though individuals over 3 metres are rarely seen. Boa constrictors can be at home in the water, though they hunt much more on land or in trees than the large anaconda. However, the smaller species of anacondas also hunt in trees. Interestingly, boa constrictors are more commonly captured than anacondas in the fish and shrimp traps placed at the river's edge along the Lower Amazon. These traps are placed during the high water period and the snakes enter them to feed on the imprisoned fish and shrimp. Their attraction to fish traps is due to the difficulty of finding other prey during the floods.

The most aggressive snakes encountered along Amazon rivers are called *pepéua* (pronounced pay-pay-oo-ah). They are members of the world's most diverse snake family, the non-venomous Columbridae. The largest *pepéua* species reaches a length of at least 2 metres. When small the *pepéua* snakes resemble the notorious and highly venomous fer-de-lance (pit viper family) and they are often mistaken for it. It is still not known, however, whether the resemblance is a type of mimicry to help protect the young from predators, though the two groups are commonly found in the same area along river banks.

When startled or molested *pepéua* snakes greatly inflate, but also flatten, the skin of the throat and neck. They also usually recoil so that the anterior part of the body is elevated. This behaviour is very reminiscent of the Asian and African cobras (*Naja*), though the latter are highly poisonous. The *pepéua* snakes are known to be one of the principal species that feeds on large toads, most of which are avoided by other animals because these amphibians possess toxic glands and secretions on their body. One of the common names of the *pepéuas*, in fact, translates as toad-eater.

The most dangerous snakes, to humans at least, found along Amazonian river banks are the pit vipers. They are called 'pit' vipers not because they might live in holes but due to the presence of a pair of heat-sensitive pits between the eyes and nostrils. In English these highly poisonous snakes are usually referred to as the fer-de-lance or bushmaster, though there are several other species as well. In the Brazilian Amazon the fer-de-lance is called the *sucururu* and the bushmaster the *jararaca*. The others are also called *jararaca*, usually with an additional adjective to identify individual species. The pit vipers hunt mostly at night, though if prey is abundant they will also kill by day. Most of the species average 1–2 metres in length and their prey is restricted to small mammals, such as rodents and marsupials, lizards and birds. They are usually only of danger to Man when accidentally stepped or sat on or when a careless hand is stuck in a hole or other place where they might be hiding. If venom is injected, however, it can be fatal.

Most of the levees along the Amazon River are now deforested because they are the highest parts of the floodplain and hence favourite sites for peasant dwellings and agricultural crops. Deforestation greatly reduces the number of animal species along a river, and this is especially noticeable on the levees and banks during the flooding season. Ground-dwelling animals found on the floodplains move to higher land as water levels rise, and this can be in the direction of the main upland or to the levees. On the levees, however, they become very concentrated because of the limited space available. The levees, in fact, are some of the best hunting areas because of the relatively high density of game.

Tortoises are one of the animal groups that occasionally gets trapped in large numbers on the levees of some Amazonian rivers, such as the Rio Madeira. There are only two tortoises in the Amazon, and one or the other of them is found almost everywhere where there is dry land. They are among the largest tortoises found on continental land masses today, though smaller than the giant tortoises found on some of the islands in the Pacific and Indian Oceans. The Amazon, and many other areas in the world, once had giant tortoises as well but these became extinct long ago.

The yellow-footed and red-footed tortoises, or *jaboti* as they are called in Brazil, colonize floodplain areas during the low water period. They follow the receding waterline eating fruits, seeds and other plant material left behind by the floods. With the floods, however, large numbers of them fail to migrate in time to the higher upland. They become marooned on levees which can become isolated as islands by the flooding waters. Man is now the major predator of *jaboti* tortoises but jaguars probably once were as the large cats stalk the levees during the floods as they know their prey becomes concentrated in this habitat.

Before leaving our discussion of river banks we will explore the most recent type to appear in the evolution of Amazonian riverine habitats – the village, town and city waterfront. To risk a pun, the Amazonian urban river bank is an offal place, to say the least. It differs most notably from other river banks in the quantity of carrion, usually consisting of discarded animal parts, and a wide variety of other types of garbage. The urban river bank is probably the habitat where black vultures are most common in the Amazon. They decorate the tops of waterfront public markets like an army of gargoyles, always ready to descend to the shore during the day to scavenge up whatever has been tossed away and is edible. They are not the most pleasant animals to watch feeding, but their role as nature's sanitary engineers cannot be underestimated. Unlike most other birds, vultures have specialized gastric juices to neutralize the bacteria that would kill most other animals. Though ugly on the ground, when soaring on long and agile wings over the waters in front of riverine towns and cities, they evoke a feeling of tranquillity.

The fish species most common around urban waterfronts are the scavengers and carrion-feeders, some of the main ones being catfish. Two groups of quite different catfish families have specialized teeth that, though small, are razor-sharp and can be used to bite out pieces of carrion flesh. An individual tooth of the *piracatinga* catfish, a species that reaches over 60 centimetres in length, has the general form of a rounded traffic sign, including its post. The round part is the cutting edge and is seated on top of a narrower base. The *piracatinga* is also fond of vegetable matter and is perhaps the most omnivorous of any Amazonian fish. Its broad feeding habits make it a good candidate for fish farming.

There are two notorious groups of fish in the Amazon and they are both called *candiru*. The larger *candiru* are sometimes called whale-catfish because they somewhat resemble cetaceans in general body form, though the largest species only reach about 25 centimetres in length. Like the *piracatinga* catfish, they are able to bite out pieces of flesh but, unlike the former, they also attack live animals, especially injured ones. Similar to red-bellied piranha behaviour, a school of these *candiru* can devour a victim very rapidly. The *piranhas* play this role in the floodplain waters whereas the *candiru* are mostly restricted to along river banks. The whale-catfish *candiru* become especially numerous near sites where fishermen are gutting their catches and throwing the innards into the water. At times the water seems to be boiling because of the voracious appetites of these fish. They will also attack large catfish that have been hooked on long lines. In this case the first individuals attack the anal area and, almost immediately, large numbers of others join in. The rapacious *candiru* eat their way through the intestines and stomach and devour the soft underside of the disadvantaged animal. They then eat the back muscles. If a catch is not brought aboard or ashore in time, all that is left is the head and a relatively clean skeleton.

The whale-catfish *candiru* also occasionally attack bathers. The wounds result in very distinctive scars. Once a *candiru* catfish bites its victim, it then rotates its body in a somewhat erratic fashion. The effect is almost that of a drill, that is, to cut deeper into the flesh. The scar resulting from these bites looks like it might have been caused by a large cigar that was extinguished on the skin.

The other group of *candiru* common along river banks are catfish of the family Trichomyoteridae. They are a very diverse group of fish, though folklore and legend usually give the impression that there is only one species. Most of the species are less than 30 millimetres long. Many of the smallest species are needle-like and they are commonly found in the gill chambers of the large catfish where they suck blood, whereas other species live on the flesh where they feed on mucus and blood.

Attacks on humans are difficult to verify because most of those reported involve the orifices of females and, understandably, there is a reluctance to show wounds. Traditionally, Indians bathed nude and female peasants in dresses without undergarments as *candiru* are little feared in most situations. Menstruating women, at least traditionally, avoided bathing in waters where *candiru* were common in fear that blood might attract the vicious fish. Orifices reportedly attacked by *candiru* include the vagina, anus, nose and ears. In folklore *candiru* are also attracted to urine. One motif in native folklore is of a *candiru* entering the penis by swimming up the stream of water of a urinating male. Fortunately this is highly improbable!

CHAPTER NINE

THE LOWER AMAZON

The feature that makes the Lower Amazon so very different from the rest of the river system is its tides. A daily cycle of tides replaces the dramatic seasonal river level fluctuations witnessed in the Amazonian Lowlands. These tides can be felt at least 1000 kilometres up the Amazon River, though that far upstream the daily ebb and flow is no more than a few centimetres at most. Only downriver of the mouth of the Rio Xingu, about 400 kilometres from the Atlantic, is there enough tidal lift to cause daily and extensive flooding of mud-flats and forests.

The ecological complexity of the tidal zone of the Amazon River system, which for the most part is called the Lower Amazon, or Baixo Amazonas, is greatly increased due to the thousands of islands, including those of the lower stretches of the southern tributaries. This island complex forms one of the great river archipelagoes in the world. Nearly all of the islands, with the major exception of the eastern half of Marajó, are only a few metres high in elevation and largely inundated twice daily with the tides. Most of the islands are covered with rainforest vegetation adapted to heavy inundation, not mangrove communities, because the volume of water travelling down the Amazon is sufficient all the year round to prevent a major invasion of saltwater.

The peripheral areas of the Lower Amazon are blanketed in floodplain or savanna grasslands. Upriver of the estuarine archipelago, much of the floodplain area between the Rio Tapajós and Rio Xingu is covered with aquatic grasses that form some of the largest natural river pasture in all of the Amazon. At the Atlantic edge of the Lower Amazon, huge savannas, studded with islands of trees, occupy the eastern half of Marajó – an island nearly the size of Scotland – and the mainland coast in the Territory of Amapá to the north. Mangroves are found along the coast and slightly up the estuarine area where seawater dominates.

In the Lower Amazon region seasonal, rather than tidal, flooding only occurs on the eastern half of Marajó. Though most of the large island is above the tidal influence, it is nevertheless inundated for about half of the year because of heavy local rainfall and poor drainage.

The Amazon River and its sediment load cannot push very far seaward because the South Equatorial Current sweeps northwards and pushes the freshwaters in that direction. The oceanic current has also prevented the Amazon from building a delta where the giant river meets the ocean, as would otherwise be expected considering the heavy sediment load. Instead the delta is hidden behind, and merges into, the western part of the large island of Marajó where a very complex and largely interconnected network of long and narrow channels cutting through alluvium form an immense wetlands area. One of these channels leads around the southeastern side of Marajó – remembering that the Amazon River flows around the northern edge – and it is for this reason that the otherwise clearwaters of the Rio Tocantins and Rio Pará are muddied before they reach the ocean.

Other than the daily fluctuations of the tides, the Amazon estuary, on either side of its northern and southern routes around Marajó, is also subject to a tidal bore, the *pororoca*. The *pororoca* is a large wave, driven by the wind but rising with the high tides (especially the equinoctial spring tides), that rolls up the estuary. As it passes over a shallow area it gains greatly in size until being swallowed eventually by deeper waters. Riding on the back of the high tide, the *pororoca* can attain a height of 3–4 metres and its crashing force tears away at alluvial banks, often undercutting them, causing the soft soil and the trees growing on it to fall into the water.

The area near the mouth of the Amazon River receives higher rainfall than the average in the Amazonian Lowlands because the daily sea breeze brings considerable moisture, hence cloud cover, with it. Heavy afternoon showers in this region can unload 20–30 millimetres of rain in less than an hour.

One of the most striking zoological features of the Lower Amazon is the large number of wading birds found in the floodplain grasslands, in the coastal savannas during the floods and in the mud-flat areas around the islands and mainland. Seldom do floodplain lakes of the Amazonian Lowlands have such large quantities of wading birds as are found in the Lower Amazon, but in part this may also be due to their decimation in the last 100 years or so as a result of game hunting and the feather trade. We know from reports written in the last century by the famous Swiss naturalist, Emile Goeldi, whose name is now given to the Goeldi Museum in Belém, that the Lower Amazon had even larger bird populations than are found at present. The feather trade was already threatening the wading bird populations, of Marajó especially, at the end of the last century.

The Lower Amazon would be a wading bird paradise – if it were not for Man, of course – because of the seasonal and daily development of huge expanses of shallow waters where there is relatively high production of food organisms, such as small fish, crabs, shrimp, mollusks, insect larvae and other invertebrates. Apart from the abundant food, wading birds are also attracted to the region because the grasslands, studded with hummocks of tree-covered islands or fringing forest, provide nesting and roosting sites.

The Amazon has a relatively rich collection of egrets and herons, though none of the species is restricted only to the basin. Many of the species reach as far as North America and some, such as the cattle egret and striated heron, are even found in the Old World as well. Large egret and heron populations are most associated with some of the muddy river floodplain lake areas and the coastal wetlands, including the eastern half of Marajó island. For, it is only in these waterbodies that they find sufficient fish and invertebrate food. Some of the species are occasionally seen along clearwater and blackwater rivers, but very rarely are more than about a dozen individuals seen together in these nutrient-poor waters.

In general the principal habitat of egrets and herons is the lake or river edge, though if waters are shallow they will feed far offshore. They move with careful steps, giving the impression that danger is always nearby. The snowy egret vibrates its feet to stir up small fish, crustaceans and other prey, whereas the little blue heron and the green heron rake their feet through the water to produce the same effect.

The Amazon has several famous egret and heron nesting regions. The largest are those of the Lower Amazon and on Marajó island. As the nesting season approaches, most of the heron and egret species display lively feather colours and their head crests become very pronounced, adding a regal demeanour to their profile. All of the species form pairs and there is much pre-nuptial screeching. The nesting colonies are usually mixed, though each species more or less defines and controls its own space within the heterogeneous assemblage of egrets, herons and even other birds. The favourite nesting sites are usually relatively large waterbodies with forest-covered islands that provide tree roosting and nesting sites. Most nesting takes place towards the end of the floods so that the young, after an incubation period of 3–4 weeks, are born as food resources become more concentrated. Food for the young is often collected far away from the nest sites, and this helps decrease the chances of predators finding the hatchlings.

When the other herons and egrets are busy feeding during the day, the boat-billed heron is resting, in a dead-still position on a shaded branch, for it is the only species of its group that is largely nocturnal. It is readily differentiated from other species by its huge eyes and large and greatly flattened beak. When the beak is pressed against its breast, as it is when it is resting, it reminds one of a Buddhist in profound meditation. As dark falls, the boat-billed heron leaves its roost and begins to fish along the water's edge.

Another foot-shuffler is the wood-stork, also called wood ibis. It is a large water bird easily identified because of its greyish-black neck, head and bill. It feeds by shuffling slowly through the shore zone, at the same time poking its beak into the water. In the muddy rivers it cannot easily see prey but detects fish, crustaceans and other small animals when they are touched with the tip of the beak.

Unlike the other storks of the region, which are gregarious and often seen crossing rivers or floodplain waterbodies in relatively large flocks, the *maguari* is usually seen alone or in pairs and is one of the few wading birds that is commonly seen along the nutrient-poor blackwater and clearwater rivers. It is, however, most abundant in the muddy river areas where prey is more plentiful. It uses its beak rather than its feet to stir up prey.

The *jabiru* stork has one of the most massive and heavy beaks of any of the Amazonian wading birds and, like the wood-stork, it has a black beak, head and neck, the latter with a ring of red where it joins the body. It stalks shallow waters by walking on what appear to be nervous feet, at the same time stabbing the water to roust prey out of hiding. With its massive beak it is able to capture relatively large fish, turtles, young caimans and other shore prey.

The mud-flats, including the mangrove areas, of the Amazon estuary provide ideal habitats for many species of crabs. A number of predators also depend on these crabs for a large part of their food. A laughter-like cry or melodious whistle means the rufous crab-hawk, a specialist on the mud-flat crabs, is in the area. The predator pounces on crabs during low tides when the crustaceans are exposed.

The snail-kite, another predator common in the mangrove areas, also attacks crabs but mollusks are also an important part of its diet. After a prey animal is captured the snail-kite takes it to a favourite perch – usually a tree that is shared by other individuals of its same species. The discarded crustacean and mollusk remains provide additional nutrients, such as calcium and phosphorus, which fertilize the water and thus increase the production of aquatic plants. Manatees, which in this area include both the Amazonian and West Indian species, are sometimes attracted to these fertilized aquatic meadows because of their rich productivity.

Three of the most beautiful animals associated with mud-flat crabs are the scarlet ibis, roseate spoonbill and flamingo, the last now very rare. The scarlet and pink colours of these birds are due to the ingestion of the pigment compounds (carotenoids) that are found in the crustaceans on which they feed.

Ibises in general differ from other Amazonian wading birds in their long, thin and curved bills. The scarlet ibis, for example, walks slowly along the water's edge with the tip of its beak submerged, at the same time constantly opening and closing the mandibles to stir up the crabs and other prey it feeds on. Crab production in the interior waters of the Amazon is probably insufficient to support scarlet ibis populations of any size. Only occasional groups appear to move any further upriver than about Santarém, 1000 kilometres from the ocean. In the Lower Amazon the scarlet ibis is known to travel over 100 kilometres in a round trip between its feeding and roosting sites, the latter usually habitats of dense vegetation away from the mud-flats.

The roseate spoonbill is an exception within the ibis family because of its massive and flattened bill which is also rounded at the end. Like the scarlet ibis, the roseate spoonbill does not move up the Amazon very far, preferring to remain near coastal mud-flat areas where it feeds on crustaceans, mollusks, fish and insects which it finds by moving its bill from side to side in the mud.

Flamingos have been known to nest in the brackish coastal areas of the Territory of Amapá, north of the Amazon River, and along the eastern part of the island of Marajó, to its south. Their columnar, almost conical, nests are constructed from mud. The young are fed on a red secretion produced in the parents' oesophagus. In addition to crustaceans and other aquatic animal food, the adults also feed on algae masses, such as diatoms, which they sift with their bills.

In the tidal mud-flats of the Lower Amazon millions of eyes stick above the water's surface like miniature submarine periscopes scanning the horizon for danger. These eyes belong to *Anableps*, the four-eyed fish, of which there are a small-scaled and large-scaled species in the Amazon estuarine area. No fish, of course, has four eyes but *Anableps* come as close to it as any, at least functionally. *Anableps* has evolved further than any other fish for simultaneous and equally functional aerial and aquatic vision.

The pupil of the eye of *Anableps* is divided into an upper and lower portion by flap-like extensions of the iris that both decrease glare and prevent the formation of double images on the retina caused by refraction of light at the water's surface. The upper pupil transmits light from the aerial visual field whereas the lower part of the pupil is utilized for aquatic vision.

Most adaptations must serve more than one purpose and this is true of the four-eyed fish's double vision. Living in the tidal waters of mud-flats exposes the fish to predators, especially birds, that can easily see it from above. The four-eyed fish, however, are not heavily attacked by birds, probably because the former easily see and flee aerial and wading predators. The four-eyed fish feed mostly during rising tide when they move close to muddy beaches and river banks, often near overhanging mangrove or flooded forest vegetation that supplies a relatively large input of insects falling into the water. In the brackish waters where four-eyed fish are found, they have few competitors for floating insects, since the characins, the principal surface insect-eating fish of the Amazon, cannot tolerate salty waters. The characins locate floating insects by looking upwards towards the surface, whereas the four-eyed fish elevate the upper part of the eye above the water and scan the surface just like a submarine periscope. In the extremely muddy waters where they live, vision through the water is very minimal and floating insects would be difficult to locate with the normal kind of fish eye. The exposed part of the eye, however, must be protected from drying, and it is for this reason that the four-eyed fish dip their heads underwater 2–4 times per minute.

One of the animals most associated with the freshwater tidal forests of the Lower Amazon is the rock-*bacu*, a large and very heavily armoured catfish. The rock-*bacu* belongs to a family of catfish (Doradidae) that are endowed with thick bony plates along the flanks of the body. Each plate, or scute, supports at least one thick spine, usually curved backwards. A lashing from one of these catfish can cause serious injury to almost any animal. Furthermore, the rock-*bacu* has incredibly thick and long dorsal and pectoral fin spines that are serrated just like a saw. The pectoral and dorsal fin spines have an inner anatomical element that allows them to be locked when they are either fully extended or closed. If a hand is carelessly placed between the pectoral fin spine and the body, and the fin is closed and locked, it is nearly impossible to break the hold before serious injury is done. The locking mechanism is probably most used in the extended position, in which case the fin spines function as spears to ward off would-be predators. Predators that get too close can also be lashed with the body spines.

Larval and young rock-*bacu* are only found in the Lower Amazon estuary region. When born these catfish are relatively naked. By the first or second year of life, however, their bodies are covered by a series of bony plates. No other Amazonian fish is so heavily protected externally as is the rock-*bacu*. All this external bone seems like a lot of weight to cart around, but one can only assume that it decreases predation. By the time the rock-*bacu* is fully ossified externally, it certainly does remind one of a rock, in weight if not exactly in appearance.

The life history of the rock-*bacu* beats to the daily pulses of the tides and the seasonal displacement westwards and eastwards of freshwater. The large catfish tolerates little saltiness and thus it is largely excluded from the brackish water zone. Though brackish water is often found in the same habitats where rock-*bacu* live in the Lower Amazon, it is always on the bottom since salty water is heavier than freshwater. The special niche into which the rock-*bacu* has evolved is feeding and breeding in the tidal flooded forests and associated plant communities. The plant communities of the tidal flooded forests, which are mostly under the influence of freshwater during the year, differ little in general aspect and species composition from those further inland. Furthermore, though their twice daily flooding regimes are very different to their seasonally inundated inland counterparts, they nevertheless fruit at about the same time, that is, during the main floods. Of the large number of fruit-eating fish, only the rock-*bacu*, and perhaps one or two other related species, have successfully colonized the tidal flooded forests of the Lower Amazon.

The main fruiting period of the tidal flooded forests of the Lower Amazon is April to July. At this time of year the rock-*bacu* feeds twice daily when it follows the high tides into the inundated forests and waits beneath trees for falling fruit. The catfish has an enormous stomach and long intestines, into which it packs huge quantities of succulent fruits during the few hours it can remain in the flooded forests before the tides ebb and it must retreat to open waters. While in the tidal flooded forests the rock-*bacu* is not only eating fruits but also dispersing their seeds, which it defecates intact.

When the fruiting season is over the rock-*bacu* lives mainly on arum leaves and mollusks. The arums of the Lower Amazon are giant philodendron-like plants whose relatively thick trunks and 2–5 metres height make them look like shrub communities, though in fact these plants are not woody but herbaceous. The arums grow in huge patches on the lowest mud-flats, and these plant communities are often almost completely covered by the daily tides. The rock-*bacu* is especially fond of new leaves which it pulls loose with its mouth. The leaves are manipulated in the mouth in such a way that they enter the stomach more or less folded. Folding the leaves allows greater quantities of them to be stuffed into the stomach.

Large adult rock-*bacu* are rarely seen in the Amazon estuary. They almost certainly would be if they were present, as fish traps, or weirs, line the tidal flooded forests to catch the fish moving into them with the tides. Large rock-*bacu*, however, are relatively common in the muddy and clearwater rivers of the Amazonian Lowlands, and they are captured in schools when migrating upstream during the low water period. Adults probably leave the estuary to decrease competition with their younger size classes for food resources. By migrating upstream the adults are able to feed in the vast flooded forests of inland waters along with many other fruit-eating fish. Mature fish return to the Lower Amazon to spawn, thus placing their young in a nursery habitat, the tidal flooded forest, in which none of the other fruit-eating fish have developed the adaptations to live.

One of the most mysterious and least known of the fish associated with freshwater swamp areas along the Amazon estuary is the cistern-catfish. Though not a true cave-dweller, since there are no caves in the Lower Amazon region, the species is nevertheless mostly known from subterranean waters, though it has been captured in open habitats as well. The first people to discover it were well- and cistern-diggers at the turn of the century who supplied specimens to the local museum. Like so many Amazonian animals, this species awaits a naturalist to study exactly what adaptations it has to live its peculiar life in subterranean waters.

Many of the areas of the estuarine islands and shores of the Amazon River and the lower reaches of the easternmost tributaries are very swampy, even during low tides. It is on these soils that the tall *Mauritia*, or *buriti* (pronounced burr-ee-tea), palm dominates and often forms almost pure stands many kilometres long. Though flooded forest plants can tolerate many months of continuous inundation, the great majority of them, unlike the *buriti* palm, are not adapted to live in soils that never dry out. The palm communities are very interesting from a biological point of view because they 'break the rule' of rainforest diversity where high densities of the same species over large areas are rare. Despite the greatly reduced plant diversity in *buriti* palm forests, they nevertheless support a large number of animal species.

The *buriti* is an elegant palm reaching about 25 metres in height. Its crown consists of a bouquet of large fronds in the shape of an opened hand-fan. The trunk is very smooth, unlike many other flooded forest palms armed with pungent spines. The *buriti* palm is so important to the local peoples that it is often referred to as the tree of life. Various parts are used for oil, wine, starch, timber, cork, fibre for weaving and tying, palm hearts and fertilizer.

Few trees in the Amazonian flooded forests have their fruits fed on by as many animal species as those of the *buriti*. In the Lower Amazon the *buriti* trees produce enormous clusters of fruits between about February and July, that is, the main rainy season. Larger trees might have upwards of 100 kilogrammes of fruit. The principal animals that attack the fruits while they are still on the tree are the macaws, parrots and parakeets. Only the macaws, however, are able to crack the large nuts, whereas the parrots and parakeets must content themselves with the outer pulp. In the *buriti* forests of the Lower Amazon the blue-and-yellow, scarlet, red-and-green, chestnut-fronted, red-bellied, and red-shouldered macaws are common, and even the hyacinth macaw enters these habitats by some of the nearby tributaries.

Not only do macaws find food in the palm forests but the *buriti* is also one of their favourite nesting sites in the eastern Amazon. The interior part of the *buriti* stem is pithy and soon begins to rot once the tree has died. The rotting process leaves hollow compartments in the stem that make ideal nesting sites for macaws, parrots and some other birds. They will hollow out these chambers further or open larger entrances to them if the outer trunk is decomposed enough to be torn apart with the beak. The rotting pith may also help to maintain relatively high and stable temperatures within the hollow, and it may also absorb, or better still drain, the nearly liquid faeces of the young.

Both female and male macaws, along with either the eggs or newborn, live together in the nest. During the nesting period they remain very quiet to prevent the unwelcome attention of potential predators. The average incubation period for macaws is between 20–30 days. It is mostly the female that incubates the eggs, while the male gathers food which he shares with her. When the eggs hatch, the newborn are largely fed by the male on nearly liquid regurgitated food. It is still not known if *buriti* fruit is used to feed the young, but this is to be expected as the tree is fruiting at the same time as the macaws are nesting.

Few predatory birds feed on fruit, but one that does, the black caracara (a type of falcon), is attracted to *buriti* forests. It is a very omnivorous feeder, taking carrion, fish, invertebrates and vegetable matter. *Buriti* pulp may well supply it with important vitamins largely missing from its other foods.

The great majority of *buriti* fruit falls on to swampy ground, or into the water, before it can be eaten by birds. Several species of large *bacu* catfish move into the *buriti* forests with the tides to feed on the fallen fruits. These catfish are probably the only animals that disperse the seeds to any extent since they are the only ones that swallow the fruits whole. There are at least 20 fish species that feed on the *buriti* fruits. The headstanders have large, rabbit-like teeth used to gnaw away the soft pulp surrounding the palm seed. Other species, especially some of the smaller characins, are unable to gnaw through the outer skin, but once it becomes softened by the water, they then feed on the accessible pulp. Along the shores or less swampy parts of the *buriti* palm forests, turtles and tortoises also gather to feed on the abundant fruit pulp which they gnaw away from the seed. Peccaries, deer, agoutis, pacas and iguanas also feed heavily on the pulp material. Caimans are reported to take the *buriti* fruits, though they probably feed more heavily on the fish that become concentrated in the pools during low tide.

The most famous and beautiful palm in the Amazon is a member of the *Euterpe* group, or the *assaí* (pronounced ah-saw-ee). It is nowhere more common than in the swampy areas of the Lower Amazon where, like the *buriti*, it often grows in large and almost pure stands along the rivers and islands. In great contrast to the *buriti*, the *assaí* has a very thin stem. The fronds are always a luscious green because, unlike most palms, the dead leaves fall to the ground immediately. *Assaí* palm forests exposed to the easterly winds blowing off the Atlantic will often have the upper stems bent westwards in a most majestic fashion. Many of the same animals that feed on the *buriti* fruits also eat those of the *assaí*. *Assaí* fruits are smaller, usually the size of a grape, purple and with a hard nut. The pulp is a thin layer surrounding the large nut. The major seed predator of the *assaí* today is undoubtedly Man, as the unfermented wine made from its thin pulp is the favourite regional drink, especially of the eastern Amazon where the juice is sold on many street corners of cities and towns and made into delicious ice creams.

Whereas *buriti* fruits are most abundant during the rainy season, those of *assaí* mature from about May to throughout the dry season, or until about December. Thus, the fruits of one or other of the two palm species are available throughout most of the year to fruit-eating animals. Macaws, parrots and ground-dwelling animals undoubtedly benefit from the largely non-overlapping fruiting seasons of the two most abundant palm species. It is not known how many animal species might disperse the seeds of each, though smaller birds, such as many parrots, fruit-eating doves, toucans and cotingas are probably important disseminators for *assaí*. The seeds of both species sink, and thus water would probably not be as good a dispersal agent as animals. The non-overlapping fruiting behaviour may have evolved so that each species would not have to compete with the other for seed-dispersal agents.

One of the reputed dispersal agents for *assaí* seeds in Amazonian folklore is the giant electric eel. Many fishermen claim to have seen the electric eel wrap around an *assaí* tree, with the express purpose, they feel, of sending a shock up the stem to the crown to dislodge the fruits and provide a meal for itself. The electric eel swallows the fruits whole and only digests the pulp. The seeds, when defecated, are then dispersed. An electrical impulse, according to the folklore, is a signal to the *assaí* that its fruits will be dispersed.

Assaí fruits are collected by skilled climbers that pull and push themselves up the thin stems with their hands and feet respectively. Folklore also claims that one of the dangers of this profession is for the *assaí* tree to be shocked during a climber's ascent. The shock reportedly carries a charge of electricity forceful enough to cause the climber to lose his grip and fall out of the tree. As the climber hits the water he is soon showered by falling *assaí* fruits, also dislodged by the shock. While in the water he is given some more shock-treatment by the eels to encourage him to stay away from *assaí* trees, thus ensuring a greater supply of food for the fish. It does appear that electric eels eat *assaí* fruits, but physicists who have been questioned feel that the palm could not conduct enough electricity to signal the fruits to drop or to shock a climber. Scientific experiments, however, are still wanting.

The eastern Amazon, along the coastal area and the mouth of the main river, is a kind of geographical gate for several animal groups that appear to have only recently, geologically speaking, entered the large river system. The scorpion mud-turtle and an emydid turtle are among this eastern Amazonian fauna. They are the only two aquatic turtle groups found in the Amazon other than the side-necked turtles discussed in the last chapter. Neither makes it very far up the Amazon river, and they have colonized areas mostly outside the main area of distribution of the side-necked turtles.

The Amazon emydid turtle is often found in habitats that dry out and which are marginal for the side-necked turtles. It is thus adapted to live a semi-terrestrial life. The emydid turtle is most notable for its giant eggs. Individuals about

20 centimetres long produce 2–4 eggs, each of which is about 7–8 centimetres long and 3–4 centimetres wide. These eggs, then, are about twice the size of those of the average chicken. The eggs are laid in shallow depressions beneath leaves. Large eggs also produce large hatchlings. Large hatchlings perhaps have a better chance at survival in the marginal, often desiccating environments where they are born.

The scorpion mud-turtle (musk turtle family), or *mussuã* as it is called locally, is the most common turtle of the extreme eastern Amazon centring on the large island of Marajó. Elsewhere in the Amazon it is relatively rare. The English name is derived from its Latin scientific name and refers to the horny, spur-like tail-tip of the male which is reminiscent of a scorpion. The strange-looking tail is not a venom organ but rather a clasper used to hold females during copulation. It is a small species, reaching only about 20 centimetres in length, and notably different from the side-necked turtles because of its hinged plastron (lower shell). When the animal is frightened, the plastron can be closed against the carapace (upper shell) to protect the soft parts. It has a relatively large head and jaws, looking somewhat parrot-like, and feeds on mollusks, insects and plants.

The scorpion mud-turtle is especially common in the low-lying savanna woodland areas of the eastern half of the island of Marajó. The large swampy area of eastern Marajó is inundated mostly by rainwater that is impounded in the low depression covering a large part of the internal island. During the rainy season the Marajó swamps teem with life as aquatic plants grow rapidly and insects, mollusks, crustaceans, fish, birds and many other animal groups flourish to take advantage of food resources. The scorpion mud-turtle is part of this rich aquatic fauna. Between September and December, however, the rains are insufficient to fill the Marajó savannas and they largely dry up, leaving only occasional lakes and waterholes. The previously verdant grasslands become dry and brittle. The scorpion mud-turtles take refuge in the tall grass of the lower-lying areas.

It is during the dry season that the scorpion mud-turtles are extremely vulnerable to Man. Turtle fire-drives on Marajó have probably been going on since Indians first arrived on the large island at least 5000 years ago. With few Indians left, the practice is continued by the peasant culture. To capture the turtles, ground is often cleared in areas downwind of where the animals are known to congregate. The dry grass is then fired and the turtles flee to the open areas where they are then captured. The scorpion mud-turtle has long been popular in the markets of Belém, the eastern Amazon's largest city, and is also one of the delicacies served in the local restaurants. Its capture has long been illegal, though to little if any effect.

Another group of animals that appears to be pushing up the Amazon River from the coastal freshwater and brackish waters is the livebearers of the family

Poeciliidae, to which belong the famous guppies. The guppies and most other members of their family are called livebearers because they are ovoviparous, that is, the eggs are fertilized and hatch internally. The males of livebearers have a highly specialized organ, the gonopodium, which is formed from anal fin rays, and acts as a kind of penis to intromit sperm into the female. Live birth may in large part be an adaptation to disperse the young to suitable habitats within precarious environments, such as tidal streams and swamps.

Guppies and other members of their family are especially common in the freshwater tidal streams and forest pools of the Amazon estuary, though some of the species also enter the brackish waters as well. Guppies have attracted much attention not only as beautiful aquarium fish but also as potential mosquito-control animals, especially in areas infested with malaria. Very few experiments, however, have been made in the Amazon to determine if guppies might help reduce urban populations of mosquitoes.

The strangest-looking animal that feeds on guppies in the Lower Amazon, especially in the freshwater tidal areas, is the *Pipa* toad. It belongs to the only Amazonian group of completely aquatic anurans, as frogs and toads together are called. The other frogs and toads only use water for breeding and during tadpole development. *Pipa* toads are so flattened in shape that they look as if they have been run over by a steamroller and then the squashed remains thrown into the water. Closer inspection, however, will reveal huge hind feet that are fully webbed to form powerful swimming paddles. The front limbs are small and terminate in star-shaped appendages that function as tactile organs for navigation and to detect prey movement in the water. *Pipa* toads lack teeth and tongue altogether. When a prey, such as a guppy, passes near to them they pop up and attempt to rake it towards the mouth. The prey will then be held with the front limbs and mouth until it can be swallowed.

Frogs and toads do not drink but absorb water through their skin. In order not to become bloated, aquatic species must limit the amount of water retained in their bodies. *Pipa* toads do this by urinating continuously. Furthermore, unlike terrestrial species, the aquatic frogs and toads excrete about 90 per cent of their waste nitrogen as ammonia, whereas in terrestrial species this is often reduced to less than 5 per cent (with a high retention of salts) so as to prevent dehydration.

Relatively few frogs or toads carry their eggs on their bodies. The *Pipa* toads are one of the major exceptions. The egg laying begins with a complicated sequence in which a male and female pair begin ascending from the bottom to the surface. At the surface they turn over in a fashion describing a loop. The female has an extendible cloaca – the posterior cavity of the genital and urinary tracts – which she uses to place the eggs topside. At the same time the male fertilizes the eggs and uses his large hind feet to manoeuvre them towards the centre of the female's back. The looping behaviour continues until all, usually about 100, eggs are laid. During the next 24 hours ridges of spongy material form around the eggs until each is almost totally embedded in its own cell. The eggs are carried on the female's back for about 100 days. During various stages of development the young toads occasionally poke various parts of their anatomy out of the egg cell, though they only leave when they are capable of free-swimming movements.

CHAPTER TEN

THE FRIGHTENED FOREST

Time and chance have been on the side of life in the Amazon, for in no other large region of the world has the diversification of species benefited so much and suffered so little from continental and global changes. From its recognizable beginnings to the present the Amazon has undergone a number of radical transformations brought on by separating continents, the appearance of flowering plants, the rise of the Andean mountains, the reversal of the main river's course and Ice Age fluctuations in temperature leading to the locking and unlocking of water at the polar ice caps. Each major transformation ushered new challenges into the Amazonian theatre of life. As each challenge was met, there was an overall increase in the number of species because of new ecological opportunities.

An abiding warm and humid climate, in contrast to the frigid periods the higher latitudes suffered and still suffer, favoured the diversification of life in the Amazon. Although extinctions undoubtedly took place, they fell far behind the ingenious ways that plant and animal species found to pack themselves even tighter into the rainforest ecosystem. There is no way of knowing whether the Amazon has reached its fullest potential in diversity, but it seems clear that neither has it ever before been so rich in species and, because of this, nor has the planet.

Modern genetics suggests that diversity is life's greatest insurance policy. Diversity begets diversity in the tropical rainforest because more biological information has been deposited in this ecosystem, through evolution's investments, than in any other gene bank in the world. This genetic information earns interest in the sense that as each species has been added to the ecosystem, the number of biological interactions increases not by a minimum of two, since every organism must interact with at least one other in order to survive, but in most cases probably by hundreds if not thousands. An individual rainforest tree species may be visited by thousands of species of invertebrates, vertebrates, fungi, bacteria and other organisms during its life. If we assume conservatively that each species interacts during its lifetime with a minimum of 100 other species, and that there is a minimum of 2 million species in the Amazon, then there are at least 200 million specific interactions between different organisms. The real number is probably closer to a billion. At present the number of interactions between species that have been identified for the Amazon probably does not exceed 10 000. Of these no more than about 100 are understood in any detail.

We noted above four great transformations the Amazon has undergone during its long history. The next major transformation, the fifth, and already under way, springs not from internal forces within the Earth, the appearance of a new class of plants or from solar system-induced changes in the polar ice caps, but rather from human economy cynically disregarding diversity. Ironically many of the changes now set in motion by human economy parallel, in their general characteristics, those that have taken place historically, though they will decrease rather than increase diversity.

When South America and Africa separated, each continent took a different evolutionary path that led to distinct faunas and floras. This resulted in a considerable increase in life's diversity because both continents were largely tropical, contained complex geographies and each had a large river basin that became covered mostly with rainforest. It is somewhat ironic that one of the greatest dangers that Amazonian diversity now faces is the Africanization of the landscape. This Africanization process sprouts from the grass seeds that are sown after cutting down the rainforest. Flowering plants conquered the Amazon with trees, not grasses. The developers of the Amazon, however, want grasses and they use mostly African species because of their robustness and aggressive colonization characteristics. The pasture philosophy has resulted in one of the largest, most expensive and uncontrolled agricultural experiments in the history of the planet. Two decades into this experiment have cost about 5 per cent of the Amazonian rainforest, damaged several important fisheries and greatly increased the poverty of the region. If you drive along the Transamazon Highway, which slices across the southern part of the Amazon and was the first focus of the rainforest-to-grassland experiment, you will not see an Amazonian John Wayne on horseback proudly viewing his herd grazing on lush pasture. Instead you will see poverty, scrawny cattle and mostly abandoned, unproductive pastureland where rainforest seedlings and African grasses are doing battle for possession of the cleared land. The river fisheries were hurt because they were written off, that is, over-exploited in the belief that cattle ranches would soon replace them as protein-producers. The pastureland focus has now shifted to the southern Amazon centred on the states of Mato Grosso, Rondônia and Acre where deforestation rates are much greater than they were along the Transamazon Highway. The burning of the rainforest has become so accelerated in this area during the dry season that it has alarmed both national and international organizations concerned with the environment. What is not usually noted, however, is that once the smoke clears each year with the beginning of the rainy season, a part of Africa sprouts up. If the African grasslands now expanding rapidly in the Amazon become too large it is highly unlikely that the rainforest could return to these areas in anything less than hundreds of years even if the uncontrolled burning were stopped.

We know that the rise of the Andes formed an enormous dam that for a few millions of years interrupted the flow of the Amazon to the ocean. Man, with the many Amazonian dams now planned, would like to match the mountains. The difference, of course, is that the Andean dam was formed over millions of years and the plants and animals had long periods of time in which to evolve the adaptations needed to survive as species or to give rise to new species. A dam built across a large river gives almost no time for the plants and animals to regroup themselves into the diverse communities in which they are found under normal, meaning evolutionary rather than revolutionary, circumstances. The most lamentable footnote to Amazonian dam building is not that the river systems are impounded – for some of them need to be for energy purposes – but the fact that they are so poorly known scientifically and almost nothing serious is done to avoid the negative effects. They are hit-and-miss operations built under the philosophy of what you don't know doesn't hurt you. They may turn out to be more damned than dammed. Their construction costs greatly increase foreign debt, which is already in financial outer space, and only multi-national corporations have the capital to build new industries which can justify the price tags of the dams. Both of these factors can lead to political unrest.

When global temperatures were warmer, the ice caps smaller and sea levels higher, the Amazon was more lake-like than at present. The burning of tropical rainforests, combined with the combustion of fossil fuel elsewhere on the planet, might possibly lead to warmer global temperatures and the partial melting of the ice caps and once again to higher sea level. When a forest is burned large quantities of carbon dioxide are released from the living vegetation and the soils associated with it. Although carbon dioxide is one of the rare gases of the air, it plays an extremely important role because it absorbs long-wave energy that is reflected from the Earth's surface. It does not, however, absorb the incoming short-wave energy, thus the process leads to warming. This phenomenon is known as the greenhouse effect. If major parts of the polar ice caps melt, some of the world's largest cities – for example, Rio de Janeiro, London and New York – would then be flooded as they are near sea level. It is an arresting thought that the collective match struck to the Amazon, along with the industrial pollution spewed into the atmosphere by North American and European countries, could be the culprit that chases Rio's carnival to higher ground, soaks Big Ben's feet after the Thames spills over its flood barriers and turns Manhattan into an urban area where gondolas will replace cars. Ironically, the interior parts of most continents would probably become drier because of warmer temperatures, despite the fact that the coastal areas would be flooded.

On the other hand, the oceans might be able to absorb all of the extra carbon dioxide caused by forest burning and industrial pollution since they can accommodate much more of this gas than the atmosphere. In this case, global temperatures might not increase to a point of melting polar ice caps and raising sea level, though no one can be sure of this in the present state of scientific knowledge. If the rainforest is destroyed, however, we can be sure that a major part of the planet's biological diversity will disappear and this is a more cogent argument for the Amazon's protection than what might happen to sea level.

Perhaps the most ironic fact of the Amazon is that the system is very poor in nutrients yet so rich in life. This holds for both the forests and most of the rivers. The rainforest, a giant nutrient reservoir, explains why so much can be made from so little. A complex network of rainforest roots allows certain kinds of fungi to drill into them and absorb carbohydrates and other food compounds. The fungi repay the favour by grabbing nutrients from the decomposing litter layer, which the rainforest roots alone cannot do very efficiently, before they are carried away by water. The fungi then channel these precious nutrients to the roots for distribution to the plant in general. When leaf, limb and stem fall, they do not injure the ecology of the rainforest, by stealing away its precious nutrients, because the nutrients are captured and returned to the vegetation. When the rainforest is removed on a large scale, however, the nutrient safety-net is punctured. The nutrients that have accumulated and recycled in the vegetation, over hundreds if not thousands of years in some cases, escape to the rivers and are largely taken away to sea.

In some respects large-scale deforestation is not unlike the borrowing policies that now add up to the incredible foreign debts that plague several of the Amazonian countries. You cannot keep borrowing without one day having to declare bankruptcy. When you cut down a large piece of rainforest and burn it you are essentially borrowing the nutrients stored in the vegetation because so few are found in the poor soils. These forest nutrients are released by the burning at a much faster rate than they would be under the normal processes of the decomposition of dead organic matter. The released nutrients are soon washed away and then more need to be borrowed, that is, more forest burned. If too large an area of the Amazon is deforested, then its countries will owe nutrient-debts that, like their financial counterparts, can never be repaid. Throwing expensive fertilizer on the land is like making painful interest payments to service the debt. The principal of the nutrient-debt, of course, is biological diversity.

There are several types of Amazonian rainforest. The most curious of these is found where the rivers invade the floodplains – the flooded forest – the focus of this book's exploration of the Amazon. The flooded forest is one of the wonders of the tropics, indeed of the planet, because where else have terrestrial, aquatic and arboreal life interacted on such a large scale. Beyond aesthetic and scientific interest the flooded forest also contains one of the great answers to how Man can benefit from the rainforest short of its wholesale destruction for quick timber or livestock profits.

The rainforest contains relatively few harvestable plants and animals. Most of the plants are not edible because high diversity has meant that each species during its evolution needed a built-in arsenal of chemical weapons to fight off innumerable potential wood, leaf and seed predators. Compared to many rainforest animals, humans have a rather weak stomach and intestinal system and there are few rainforest seeds and almost no leaves that they can eat. For Man, then, the rainforest is not an orchard or garden and the fruits in general are indeed forbidden.

Likewise, the rainforest is not a natural farmyard because most of the animal production is not acceptable as food. The rainforest floor and trees support a relatively small quantity of animals that can be harvested, mainly because insects, the largest part of the animal production, are not accepted as food in most societies. Humans prefer vertebrate animals as protein food rather than, say, ants and termites. This brings us back to the flooded forests.

Of the food animals accepted by Man, fish are by far the most successful and productive of the Amazonian rainforest. The flooded forest, of course, is the ecological link between fish and forest. The principal reason why fish are so abundant in the rainforest compared to other vertebrate animals is their extremely high diversity which allows them, as communities, to feed on many different kinds of food. Unlike Man, communities of fish can forage on rainforest fruits, seeds, insects, leaves and detritus, all of which are abundant during the floods. Also, being cold blooded they use relatively little energy compared to mammals or birds and thus turn more of what they eat into flesh. In addition to these advantages, fish are also easier to capture on a tonnage basis than other Amazonian rainforest animals because of the large schools they form in the rivers and lakes at certain times of the year. The floodplains, with their fish and forests, offer one of the most outstanding opportunities to use the tropical jungle in a rational and productive way and, at the same time, help preserve the unique diversity of life that was born from the seasonal intercourse of water and trees.

INDEX

Bold page numbers refer to illustrations.

A

Adenomera frog, 104
agouti, 18–19
Amazon
  area of, 22
  beaches, 156–60, 177–9
  blackwater rivers, 14–15,
    40–1, 180
  clearwater rivers, 14, 180
  dam building, 201
  depths, 13–14, 21, 99–
    100
  discharge, 15–16
  floating meadows, 100–12
  flooded forest (*igapó*), 21–
    4, 28–30, 52, 54–6
  floodplain forest, **44–5**,
    71
  flow direction, 12–14
  geological development,
    11–13
  lakes, 12, 129–40
  length, 16
  levees, 179–80, 183
  and pasture philosophy,
    200–1
  sediments, 14–15, 147,
    187

  soil quality, 14–15, 202–3
  species, 12, 16–20, 54–5,
    65, 70
  tidal zone, 186–98
  tributaries, 13–15, 19,
    149
  urban waterfronts, 184
  weather systems, 130–1,
    187
  whitewater rivers, 14,
    40–1
Amazon/Atlantic interface,
    15–16, 147, 151, 186–7
Amazonian Lowlands, 14–
  15, 129
amphibians *and see* by name,
  17, 54–5
Anableps fish, 190–1
anaconda, 17, 142, 156, **169**,
  181–2
Andes, origins of, 12–13, **38**
Annona plant, 25
anteaters, 18, 78–9
ant-plants, 27–8
ants, 27–8, 182
armadillos, 18
arowhana (*aruanã*) fish, 28–
  30, **88**, **121**
arums, 58, 192
assaí palm, 194–5
Atlantic/Amazon interface,
    15–16, 147, 151, 186–7

Azteca ant, 27–8

B

bacu catfish, 194
bananas, 20
barn owl, 66–7
bats, 18–19, 67–8
beach habitats, **41**, 156–60,
  177–9
bees, 24–5
beetles, 25, 101, 103
birds *and see* by name, 18
  beach habitats, 159–60,
    177
  diving, 181
  fish-eating, 139–40
  fruit-eating, 59, 62, 193–
    4
  gallinaceous, 56, 59
  ground-dwelling, 56–7
  lake habitats, 139–40
  migratory, 18, 139–40,
    159–60
  predatory, 65–6, 140,
    189, 194
  in rainforest, 55–6
  in river meadows, 102–3
  and seed dispersal, 62, 63
  seed-eating, 59, 60
  species numbers, 18, 54–
    5, 65

PICTURE CREDITS

ARDEA pages 35 *bottom right* (K. & L. Laidler), 43 (Adrian Warren), 47 *bottom* (Adrian Warren), 84 *top left* (François Gohier) & 169 *bottom* (K. & L. Laidler); MARCIO AYRES page 172–3 *right*; JIM CLARE pages 44–5, 81, 84 *bottom left*, 162–3 *left*, 164–5, 168 *bottom* & 172 *bottom left*; BRUCE COLEMAN pages 33 (Rod Williams), 35 *top right* (Luiz Claudio Marigo), 38 *bottom* (Jeff Simon), 40–1 *left* (Luiz Claudio Marigo), 41 *right* (Michael Freeman) & 161 (H. Rivarola); ANDREA FLORENCE pages 88 *top*, 113, 114 *bottom*, 120 *both*, 124–5 *both* & 176 *both*; JENNIFER FRY page 46; MICHAEL GOULDING pages 38 *top*, 48 *both*, 88 *bottom*, 92 *bottom*, 114 *top*, 115, 121 *both*, 126–7, 167 *right*, 169 *top*, 170–1 & 164–5; HUTCHISON LIBRARY page 42 *both* (Jesco von Puttkamer); LUIZ CLAUDIO MARIGO pages 34–5 *left*, 36–7, 82, 84–5, 86–7, 90–1, 92 *top*, 95 *bottom right*, 118 *top*, 119, 128, 168 *top* & 175 *right*; RUSSEL A. MITTERMEIER pages 94–5 *left* & 116–17; TONY MORRISON, SOUTH AMERICAN PICTURES pages 47 *top* & 83; NHPA pages 39 (Martin Wendler), 89 (Agence Nature), 93 (Jany Sauvanet), 96 (Jany Sauvanet), 122–3 (John Shaw), 163 *right* (Jany Sauvanet) & 166–7 *left* (Martin Wendler); OXFORD SCIENTIFIC FILMS page 95 *top right* (Michael Fogden); HARVEY SHERMAN page 118 *bottom*.